The NEC Engineering
and Construction Contract
A user's guide

Jon Broome

⊥ᵀ Thomas Telford

Published by Thomas Telford Publishing, Thomas Telford Ltd, 1 Heron Quay, London E14 4JD.
URL: http://www.t-telford.co.uk

Distributors for Thomas Telford books are
USA: ASCE Press, 1801 Alexander Bell Drive, Reston, VA 20191-4400
Japan: Maruzen Co. Ltd, Book Department, 3–10 Nihonbashi 2-chome, Chuo-ku, Tokyo 103
Australia: DA Books and Journals, 648 Whitehorse Road, Mitcham 3132, Victoria

First published 1999

A catalogue record for this book is available from the British Library

ISBN: 0 7277 2750 8

Throughout the book the personal pronouns 'he', 'his', etc. are used when referring to 'the Contractor', 'the Employer', etc. for reasons of readability. Clearly it is quite possible these hypothetical characters may be female in 'real-life' situations, so readers should consider these pronouns to be grammatically neuter in gender, rather than masculine.

Typeset by Ian Kingston Editorial Services, Nottingham, UK
Printed and bound in Great Britain by The Cromwell Press, Trowbridge, Wiltshire

Foreword

As a Chartered Civil Engineer since 1975 and having worked in a construction client organisation since leaving secondary school in 1964, I have fulfilled all of the roles within a contract, from site engineer to the Engineer and the Employer's Representative. From almost the outset, even in my university studies on contract administration, I have been struck by the manner in which construction contracts are produced and by the behaviour typically displayed by the main players.

The New Engineering Contract (NEC) seemed completely different to other standard forms when I first encountered it in 1992, and I could see what it was aiming to achieve. I was able to influence my own company, London Underground Limited (LUL), and we began to use it in earnest from 1995/96 onwards. By 1999 some £500 million plus value of work had been committed under the NEC.

LUL, as with many other clients to the construction industry, have experienced the problems of overrun that have become so commonplace on construction projects. Of all the parameters, time is the most important to us. The good management of time is vital to a client who has an operational business, since loss of time on a construction project will invariably have a consequential and detrimental impact on the client's main business.

While the more traditional standard forms of contract contain some guidance on contract management methodology they clearly have not been written and constructed with best practice contract management in mind. To address this issue of programme control and cost management an approach is needed which gives guidance and sets down a complete framework for good contract administration. It is unfortunate but true that people often need greater encouragement than simply being asked to behave in a certain way. If one accepts that, then a contract form which makes best practice a contractual obligation, and has sanctions on both parties for not meeting these obligations, is more than a step in the right direction.

The NEC is built around good contract management practice. At its heart is the important concept of managing time, i.e. planning and programming. It is said that to control time is to control cost. The NEC contains clear requirements for producing and updating the programme; all changes are required to be addressed in terms of effect on time and cost. The obligations built into the contract place requirements on both parties to perform in a timely manner. The client (or his representative) is required to give timely information and make decisions within a set timescale. The contractor is required to properly plan and replan the works as it progresses.

After the first year of use, LUL had a review conducted by an outside practice, taking the views of all involved on its NEC contracts, including contractors and consultants. Out of this review, the most impressive piece of feedback, from all concerned, was that the principles and objectives were seen as good and were thoroughly supported. However, while the warnings of existing users, the drafters and training bodies had been heard, they clearly had not been fully appreciated. There were many successes, but it was clear that training, preparation, management leadership and other such aspects were in need of improvement, and by all parties. These have since been addressed.

It has been said that the NEC is a 'demanding' contract form which requires discipline of all involved; it is now much better understood what is meant. Good contract management is not something which happens by chance. With good discipline and contract management the need for adversarialism falls away and the contract is well managed.

The NEC is now LUL's preferred form of contract. Indeed the 'Alliancing' project (which commenced in May 1999) on LUL's Circle and District Lines near High Street Kensington is under the NEC and the £100 million plus project to be managed by LUL for the CTRL related works at Kings Cross is also planned to be under NEC, Target Cost Option D.

Therefore, training and preparation are the key to a successful application of the NEC and to the benefits it can bring to a project. In this respect, this book by Jon Broome is a major contribution to 'getting it right'. It is well written and will be of great benefit to all users, both the novice and the more experienced user. I commend it thoroughly.

Richard Bliss, BSc (Hons), Ceng, MICE
Chairman, ICE, NEC User Group 1997–99

Acknowledgements

This book is the result of four years of research, so the first people to thank are all the individuals and companies who gave their time in contributing to the research. Secondly, the author would like to state his appreciation to the organisations which funded the research: the Engineering and Physical Sciences Research Council, National Power plc and London Underground Limited. Additionally, the author would like to thank the practitioners who reviewed and commented on this work: Andrew Wrightson of National Power plc and Mike Attridge of Ellenbrook Consulting Ltd.

Gratitude is also expressed to my colleagues in the School of Civil Engineering at The University of Birmingham. A special thank you to Professor John Perry, for his time and patience during the research and for his efforts in 'moulding' me and my thought processes. Also, I would like to thank David Hoare for his comments and interest in this piece of work and Ross Hayes for his general helpfulness.

Lastly, this book, like my PhD thesis is dedicated to the memory of my two grandfathers, James Broome and Percy Long, for their kindness and support throughout their lives and beyond.

project. In so doing, it attempts to tread a fine line between sufficient tightness, so that contract participants follow the procedures, and sufficient looseness so that it can be interpreted in a way appropriate to the situation encountered. Research would indicate that the authors of the ECC have been largely successful, but it does require a fundamental change in attitudes from those who will use the contract and from lawyers who advise and will eventually be involved in any litigation on the contract.

A number of commentators have noted that the NEC is as much a manual of project management as a set of conditions of contract. One of the consequences of this is that the ECC encourages up-front discussion of how situations will be dealt with. One practising lawyer[*] noted that 'if the NEC is examined with a view to ascertaining whether it provides for the rights and obligations of the parties in every imaginable situation and in view of the latest developments in the law of contract and tort, then it may be regarded as lacking. If by contrast the NEC is examined to ascertain whether its procedures stimulate good project management then it is likely to fare favourably'.

In practice, the majority of participants have grasped this change in emphasis, with one participant describing it as an 'enabling document, rather than a prescriptive document' that 'forms a framework which you interpret depending on the situation and with whom you are dealing'. However, a few interviewees within the research sample, generally on the less successfully implemented NEC contracts, have not realised this or realised it too late.

1.2.5 Conclusions on clarity

Despite the reservations of those in the legal profession, the research found that, once the learning curve was overcome, the NEC/ECC

---

[*] Herga R. H. (1995). *A management tool rather than a clear legal statement of the parties' rights and obligations — Aspects of the NEC Engineering and Construction Contract examined.* MSc thesis in Construction Law and Arbitration, Centre of Construction Law and Management, King's College London.

offers improved clarity, both procedurally and in terms of brevity. However, it is suggested that a potential user of the ECC needs not only to give each clause sufficient consideration to understand its meaning and implications, but also to reconsider how they can best be implemented in practice and the purpose of conditions of contract: to more define the relationship and processes between the parties as opposed to their rights and obligations in every conceivable circumstance.

1.3 FLEXIBILITY

If one looks at modern trends in construction procurement we find the following.

- A movement away from the use of bills of quantities towards method-related bills of quantities (e.g. CESMM 3) and more recently towards milestone payments, activity schedules and payment schedules with interim payment based on progress achieved, rather than quantity of work done.
- A recent trend towards partnering, increased use of cost-based contracts (where the Contractor is paid his site costs plus a fee) and hence open book accounting. This leads to greater transparency. When target cost contracts are used, where cost over or under runs are shared in pre-agreed proportions, it is in both parties interests to reduce costs creating an alignment of objectives.
- A movement towards management-based contracts, where the Employer employs an organisation to manage the individual works contractors on its behalf. This organisation is employed for its management expertise and does little, if any, of the physical work itself. In the late 1980s the management contracting approach, where all the works contracts are let through the management contractor was popular. More recently management contracting has been largely superseded by the construction management approach, where all the works

contract are let between the Employer and works contractors, but are administered on behalf of the Employer by the construction management organisation.

- Greater Contractor involvement in design, with the use of design and build/construct contracts, performance specifications, turnkey projects and build, operate, transfer projects.
- Increasing numbers of multi-disciplinary projects, involving civil engineering works, building works, mechanical and electrical services and expensive process plant.
- An increasingly global market for construction services, with foreign contractors entering the British market and British contractors competing on a worldwide basis.

The ECC was written with the intention of providing sufficient flexibility to accommodate these developments.

The aim of this section is to give readers an understanding of contract strategy and to outline how the ECC accommodates different contract and procurement strategies. It expands considerably on the appropriateness of different contract strategies given in the ECC Guidance Notes.

It should be noted that the development of the appropriate contract strategy for a particular project is as much an art as a science. It also has to take into account external factors, such as the availability of expertise, both technically and managerially, in both the Employers' and potential Contractor's organisations. It involves an evaluation of the risks and constraints operating on the project and includes issues such as contractor selection and tendering procedure, which are independent of the use of the ECC. Consequently, there is rarely, if ever, a perfect contract strategy, merely an optimal or 'best fit' one. If the contract strategy is inappropriate, then the contract will be set up with a high potential for failure. This was observed on a few of the contracts within the research sample. However competent the participants were, regardless of the goodwill between them and the effectiveness of the mechanisms of the NEC/ECC in stimulating good management, the contracts were effectively set up for trouble. Therefore, potential users of the ECC are advised to seek professional guidance in this respect, especially if adopting one of the less familiar contract strategies.

Further reading
A good general introduction is

The Association For Project Management Specific Interest Group on Contracts and Procurement (1998). *Contract strategy for successful project management: a guide for project managers on best practice for the procurement of goods and services.* High Wycombe, The APM Group Ltd.

1.3.1 Overview of the main options

The ECC has six main options one of which must be chosen. These are

- Option A: priced contract with activity schedules
- Option B: priced contract with bills of quantities
- Option C: target contract with activity schedules
- Option D: target contract with bills of quantities
- Option E: cost reimbursable contract
- Option F: management contract.

These options govern how the Contractor is paid. Whatever main option is chosen, many of the procedures and systems necessary to administer the contract will be the same as approximately 85% of the text is independent of the main option chosen. To further refine the contract strategy, appropriate secondary options can be chosen.

1.3.1.1 Priced contracts: Options A and B
Priced contracts are normally only used when the Employer can provide the Contractor with a complete description of what is required at the outset, so that the Contractor can price it with a reasonable degree of certainty. This does not necessarily mean a complete design, but could be a full and unambiguous statement of what is wanted e.g. as a performance specification or scope design and a statement of the purpose of the asset.

Bills of quantities are the normal payment mechanism for work procured under the traditional/sequential procurement method, where the works are substantially designed by or on behalf of the Employer before being put out to tender by Contractors. However, bills of quantities have some fundamental flaws, the biggest being that construction costs are rarely directly proportional to quantity. The effect of this flaw may be minimal if changes in the scope of the works are few as the difference between the Contractor's costs and income will remain small. Use of method-related charges[*] increases the change in scope that can be accommodated. However, friction often results when significant changes in scope or methods occur, as the Contractor struggles to justify any additional entitlement and to show where his extra costs come from. The situation is not helped by the lack of programming provisions in traditional conditions of contract.

Activity schedules are an attempt to move away from the problems associated with the use of bills of quantities. In concept, an activity schedule is similar to a series of bars on a bar chart (Gantt chart). The difference is that each bar/activity has a price attached to it and the Contractor is paid for each completed activity at the assessment date following its completion. The activity schedule is therefore closely linked to the programme and, as the Contractor prepares the construction programme, the Contractor would normally prepare the activity schedule. He would then also know his expected cash flow. An example of an activity schedule is given in Fig. 1.

The research found that the theoretical advantages which the use of activity schedules should give appeared to materialise in practice. These advantages (and some potential disadvantages) are briefly given below.

- Any significant level of *Contractor*[†] design is more easily accommodated, as design itself can become an activity. Standard

[*] Method-related charges are where the Contractor separates fixed and time related charges from quantity related costs when returning his tender.

[†] Italics are used in this book when using terminology that is specific to the NEC ECC and which are in italics in the NEC ECC. When used in a general sense, these characters are in ordinary typescript.

REF	Activity	Price (£)
A001	Mobilisation	5000·00
A002	Site clearance and establish at shaft B worksite	10 000·00
A003	Sink shaft B	63 000·00
A004	Set up pipe jack equipment in shaft B	6500·00
A005	Pipe jack shaft B to A	47 500·00
A006	Site clearance and establish at shaft A worksite	3000·00
A007	Sink shaft A	51 000·00
A008	Site clearance and establish at shaft C worksite	4000·00
A009	Sink shaft C	48 000·00
A010	Set up pipe jack equipment for drive B to C	3500·00
A011	Pipe jack shaft B to C	102 000·00
A012	Establish worksite in the Dell	2500·00
A013	Construct outfall to river — excavation and concrete works	7500·00
A014	Take delivery of *Employer*-supplied pipes to the Dell	150·00
A015	Construct 600 dia drain in Dell — open cut portion	6000·00
A016	Construct heading for drain to shaft A	17 500·00
A017	Gas diversion by Others — liaison	50·00
A018	Take delivery of *Employer*-supplied pipes at shaft C worksite	200·00
A019	Construct 600 mm dia. drain between shaft C and existing sewer	39 000·00
A020	Remove pipe jack equipment from Shaft B	1000·00
A021	Air tests	1500·00
A022	Benching, ladders, miscellaneous internal works to shafts	10 500·00
A023	Connect to existing sewer	7500·00
A024	Demobilise	4000·00
	Total £	434 150·00

Fig. 1. Activity schedule for West Drayton stormwater relief storage tunnel

methods of measurement normally assume the work is fully designed. If design is not finalised at tender, then any bill of quantities which might be prepared are, strictly speaking, not in accordance with the method of measurement: at best, they are not complete and at worst provide an opportunity for 'contractual games'.

• *Contractors* have to plan the job before they prepare their *activity schedule*. Because they start from a blank sheet, rather than being given a prepared bill of quantities, *Contractors* are forced to prepare a more thorough tender giving greater confidence in their tendered total of the Prices. This, however, is a time consuming operation, and it increases the man-hours needed to prepare a tender. Consequently, *Employers* may wish to put potential work out to fewer tenderers, in order not to push up the overheads of the industry, which they ultimately pay for (see section 3.1.4 for further discussion on this point).

- As payment is linked to completion of an activity or group of activities, the cash flow requirements for both parties are more visible.

- In order to receive payment as planned, the *Contractor* has to complete an activity by the assessment date. Consequently, he has to programme realistically and is motivated to keep to that programme during construction. Throughout the contract, the *activity schedule* should mesh with the time, method and resource documents (the Accepted Programme).

- *Contractors* are not paid for changes in quantity of the permanent work, unless an instruction changing the original specification is issued. This transfers some risk to the *Contractor*.

- The assessment of the effect of a compensation event is easier with *activity schedules* than with a bill of quantities. While the assessment is easier and fairer, because any change in resources or methods associated with an activity can be compared with those stated in the Accepted Programme before the compensation event occurred, it is a more rigorous process than using bill rates and therefore takes longer. For this reason, both parties may be happy to use a straight bill rate for the assessment of a simple compensation event. However, using straight bill rates ignores the delay and disruption costs associated with any change, which are often assessed as a claim after construction has finished, and which research has found, on average, costs approximately twice the direct costs.[*]

---

[*] Revay S. G. (1992). Can construction claims be avoided? In Fenn P. and Gameson R. (eds), *Construction Conflict and Resolution*. E & FN Spon.

- Assessment of the amounts due to the *Contractor* with an *activity schedule* is easier and involves many less person hours than with a *bill of quantities*. This and the preceding point may well account for a general feeling among participants on completed projects that the total administrative and management input from commencement of construction to settlement of final account is slightly less with priced contract with activity schedules (Option A) compared with a conventional contract form, and slightly more with the priced contract with bills of quantities (Option B).

When considering which of the priced options to use, the author therefore suggests that Option B be used when specific circumstances warrant it and not just because bills of quantities are traditionally used on contracts of that nature. Because of the practical advantages of *activity schedules* over *bills of quantities*, there has been a definite shift away from Option B towards Option A by more experienced users.

1.3.1.2 Cost reimbursable contract: Option E

Under Option E of the ECC, the *Contractor* is reimbursed his Actual Costs plus a Fee. Actual Cost for non-subcontracted work is defined in the Schedule of Cost Components at the back of the contract and predominantly covers the *Contractor's* direct and indirect on-site costs. The Fee is calculated by applying a percentage, tendered by the *Contractor*, to Actual Cost and needs to cover his off-site overheads, profit and insurances together with anything else not listed in the Schedule of Cost Components. It therefore gives little incentive for Contractors to minimise costs once on-site (unless there is an overarching business arrangement whereby the incentive is repeat order business e.g. a framework agreement). This particular strategy may be appropriate where

- time or quality are overriding priorities for the *Employer*, or
- the scope is not sufficiently defined at the outset or the contract is subject to a high level of uncertainty e.g. in planning interfaces or

risks encountered such that the *Contractor* is unable to price the works with any degree of accuracy.

An advantage of cost reimbursable contracts is that the open book accounting procedures act as a catalyst to openness in other aspects of contract administration and management.

1.3.1.3 Target contracts: Options C and D

Target cost contracts are a development of cost reimbursable contracts and are often used in less extreme circumstances to them e.g. where the scope is sufficiently developed for the Contractor to put an approximate price to it, but which still requires some development. Once under way, the *Contractor* is reimbursed his Actual Costs plus a Fee in the same way as in the cost reimbursable option. However, any cost over or under run to the agreed target (or Prices in ECC terminology) is split between the *Contractor* and *Employer* in pre-agreed proportions. Target cost contracts therefore align the motivations of the parties to decrease costs very effectively. They are increasingly being used due to the trend towards partnering, both for term and project-specific partnerships. Their use may be appropriate in the following circumstances

- when the scope of the works is not fully defined at the outset
- when a high level of flexibility for design changes is anticipated
- where both parties can contribute to decreasing the Actual Costs of construction. (For example, through the use of value management and engineering techniques.) This and the previous two points imply that there is scope for the Contractor to contribute to the development of the design.
- for sharing risk where both parties can contribute to the management of the major risks. If the Contractor was allocated the risks e.g. in a priced contract, he would put a high risk premium in his tender. The Employer may not wish to pay for risk which does not eventuate, but does wish to motivate the Contractor to manage it, or

- any combination of the above including being the means for aligning motivations in partnering relationships.

However, greater Employer involvement is essential in this contractual arrangement and unfamiliar administrative procedures, which include open book accounting, may lead to higher administrative costs. They are therefore less likely to be as suitable for low value contracts.

In the same way that priced contracts need a method of adjusting the Prices if an event for which the Employer is liable occurs (a compensation event in the ECC), so target cost contracts need a mechanism for adjusting the target Prices. In the ECC, the mechanism for evaluating the change in Prices is identical whatever the main option chosen, be it a priced contract, cost reimbursable or target options (section 1.4). However, it should be noted that with target cost contracts, like priced contracts, there is a temptation for the Contractor to maximise the financial assessment of compensation events, so as to maximise the difference between the final target Prices and final Actual Costs, thus maximising his share of the savings. In this respect, they do not align the motivations of participants. If the scope and value of the works is changed too much and too often, so that the changes are assessed retrospectively, then they can effectively revert to cost reimbursable contracts.

Further reading

Perry J. G. and Thompson P. A. (1982). *Target and cost-reimbursable construction contracts — Part A: a study of their use and implications.* CIRIA Report 85, Construction Industry Research and Information Association, London.

Perry J. G., Thompson P. A. and Wright M. (1982). *Target and cost reimbursable construction contracts — Part B: management and financial implications.* CIRIA Report 85, Construction Industry Research and Information Association, London.

Note: This is also a current research topic of this book's author, where the knowledge in the above reports is being updated to take account of partnering and expanded to investigate the subtleties involved in setting the share profiles.

1.3.1.4 Management based contracts: Option F and the Professional Services Contract (PSC)

Management based contracts are generally suitable

- where there is a need to co-ordinate a considerable number of works contractors and suppliers
- when the Employer does not have sufficient staff and/or expertise to manage the procurement of the asset themselves
- when the time scale of the project is tight, necessitating an early start of construction. The key point is that the scope of the project is not fully developed, so a price for the full works could not be accurately determined at tender, but the price for the initial works packages can be. As the scope is developed and construction progresses, successive works contracts are let and the interfaces between these packages are managed.

Management contracting, where the works contracts are let between the management contractor and works contractors, is enacted by using Option F of the ECC. In it, design, construction and installation are expected to be subcontracted leaving the *Contractor* to concentrate on the management of the works. The *Contractor* is paid Actual Costs, which includes payments to subcontractors plus a Fee, which, in the ECC, is calculated by applying a tendered *fee percentage* to the *Contractor's* Actual Costs. The management contracting approach peaked in popularity in the 1980s, being largely superseded by the construction management approach, where all the works contract are let between the Employer and works contractors. The works contracts are then administered on behalf of the Employer by a construction management company. The rise in popularity of construction management came about for a number of reasons.

- Works contractors, under the construction management approach, are less inhibited in making their design contribution and are more committed to the Employer's objectives.

- Under the management contracting approach, Employers tended to assign more and more risk to the management contractor, which he can neither manage nor price. The Contractor would thus be tempted to both pass this risk down to the works contractors and to adopt a defensive stance to minimise his potential liabilities. This undermines the objective of less adversarialism compared with the unambiguously professional role of the construction manager.
- It is more clear that the Employer retains risks under the construction management approach, especially that of default by a works contractor.
- The direct contracts between the Employer and works contractors can encourage early payment, which enhances the likelihood of good site relationships and higher productivity, leading to lower bids and potential long term relationships.
- If the relationship between the Employer and construction manager breaks down during the contract, he can terminate the contract and retain the works contractors. Under the management contract, he would have to somehow novate or assign the original works contracts to a new management contractor.

The above explain why the construction management approach has become more accepted as a better alternative to management contracting in most, but not all, circumstances, including for use with the ECC.

To use the construction management approach, Employers should let the construction management and design only contracts on the PSC and the works packages on the ECC. A problem with the ECC is that, due to its emphasis on pre-planning, the provisions of the contract may be inappropriate where the co-ordination of works contractors cannot be planned at the time of letting the individual works package. Related to this is the fact that the ECC does not contain provisions for set off, so if one works contractor delays a second works contractor, then the second may notify a compensation event and be entitled to additional time and cost, which the Employer cannot claim back from the first works contractor. It is therefore suggested that some amendments to the ECC may be necessary if the construction management approach is adopted.

Further reading

Thompson P. A., Perry J. G. and Hayes R. W. (1983). *Management contracting*. CIRIA Report 100, Construction Industry Research and Information Association, London.

University of Reading (1991). *Construction management forum: report and guidance*. Centre for Strategic Studies in Construction, Reading.

1.3.2 Secondary options

Secondary option clauses are used to further tailor the contract strategy. The choice of secondary option for use with a particular main option is illustrated in Fig. 2 on page 16 of the ECC Guidance Notes. Those justifying comment in addition to that set out in the Guidance Notes are as follows.

Performance bond (Option G) and parent company guarantee (Option H)

The objective of performance bonds or parent company guarantees is to give Employers recourse to a third party for additional costs should the Contractor fail to perform or go into liquidation. The performance bond is more commonly used because payment, in the event of the Contractor's default or insolvency, is not conditional upon its parent company being

- able to pay. A bank or similar institution has more guaranteed security. For instance, the subsidiary may be trading profitably, but its parent company may not be.
- willing to pay, as it is more likely to take the side of its subsidiary and dispute the payment.

25

However, the Contractor will have to pay a sum of money to the institution holding a performance bond, which may result in a slightly higher tender Price.

Advanced payment to the Contractor (Option J)
This option is appropriate when the *Contractor* will incur significant expenditure before doing any of the physical work. For instance, in specialist work, this might be buying a specialist piece of construction plant (Equipment in ECC terminology). In overseas work, this might be transporting Equipment to the country.

Limitation of the Contractor's liability for his design to reasonable skill and care (Option M)
Without this clause, the standard of liability in the ECC is generally taken to be fitness for purpose for which *Contractors* find it hard to obtain insurance. This option reduces it to reasonable skill and care for design which matches the standard to which a design consultancy would normally work and is able to obtain insurance for.

Bonus for early Completion (Option Q)
Research, both in human behaviour and in construction, has found that people and organisations respond better to positive rather than negative motivation. If the Employer is to receive benefit from early use of the asset, then it is worth considering giving some of this benefit to the Contractor, thus aligning motivations and increasing the likelihood of the Employer's time objective being achieved.

Delay damages (Option R) and low performance damages (Option S)
What are referred to as liquidated damages in other construction contracts are called delay damages in the ECC as they apply to time delays. Low performance damages can only be applied where performance specifications are used. While damages for a number of performance criteria can be set, they must be specific, measurable and achievable. The performance criteria must also be within the

Contractor's control. All damages must be set at a level which is a genuine pre-estimate of the financial damage which will be suffered by the Employer should the asset fail to perform, otherwise they will be construed as a penalty and be inadmissible in law. Therefore, the Employer should have detailed justification of how the rate was set and if in doubt, damages should be set low. Their other purpose is to limit the liability of the Contractor, as, if none are present, he could be liable for unlimited damages! Some Contractors, especially in the process sector, insist that low performance damages are included in the contract for this reason.

Trust Fund (Option V)

The Trust Fund option was written in response to Latham's recommendation[*] that they be used as a means of ensuring payment down the contractual chain should one party go bust. However, if used, the *Employer* has to keep one and a half times the average monthly expenditure during the contract in the trust account and maintain it at this level for the duration of the contract. If the trust account is drawn on, it has to topped up and could, therefore, become a bottomless pit. Consequently, it is rarely, if ever, used.

Additional conditions of contract (Option Z)

This option allows additional conditions to be added to further tailor the contract strategy. Amendments have also been included in an Appendix to the Contract Data. The flexibility inherent in the NEC system is designed so that amendments to the contract are kept to a minimum. However, those contemplating additional conditions should

- beware of so doing without considerable thought on how they will impact on the procedures within the contract
- do so in line with the principles of the ECC, i.e. do not

---

[*] Latham M. (1994). *Constructing the team — final report of the government/industry review of procurement and contractual arrangements in the UK construction industry.* HMSO, London.

o   clutter up the contract with minor issues which are unlikely
    to ever eventuate
o   undermine the stimulus to good management
o   undermine the drafting philosophy of the ECC by attempting
    to prescribe an outcome for every foreseeable eventuality,
    rather than a process for project managing a problem.

1.3.3 Contractor *design*

There are a number of reasons for allocating design to a contractor.

* Single point responsibility for the delivery of the project. The
  Contractor, having been given the brief, is now responsible for
  design and construction which should result in fewer compensation events.
* The design and construction periods can overlap, leading to
  faster delivery of the end asset.
* The Contractor can utilise his ingenuity and knowledge of methods
  of construction and price of materials etc. to minimise costs.
* He is more capable of managing the design risk, which results in
  greater certainty of the time, cost and performance objectives
  being met. The Employer therefore has to satisfy himself that the
  Contractor is fully capable of managing this risk.

However, if the Employer, having let the contract, then changes his
mind about his requirements, either because he has not thought them
through properly or has expressed them unclearly and ambiguously,
then this certainty is threatened and it will cost the Employer dear. As
one distinguished lawyer[*] wrote, the Employer has to learn to 'let go'
once the contract is let on any design and build contract.

In the ECC, *Contractor* design is accommodated in clauses 20, 21
and 22. Such is the flexibility of the ECC that the *Employer* can

---

* Capper P. N. (1996). 'Constructing the Team' for Procurement Reform in the Engineering
and Construction Industry using the New Engineering Contract. Paper presented at CSIR
Conference Centre, Pretoria.

- give a scope and outline design, a statement of the purpose of the asset to be constructed and refer to the standards to which it has to be constructed
- specify the performance requirements of the asset. For example, if the *Employer* wants a power station, the output, efficiency, control, environmental standards etc. that it has to conform to would be stated and the *Contractor* allowed to design and build the facility on the specified site.
- design the works himself or through a third party i.e. a design consultant, or
- use any combination of the above. For example, if he required a building he could describe the purpose of the asset and give an outline design, state the performance requirements for the mechanical and electrical services, yet retain control for key parts of the asset e.g. an architectural feature, by designing it himself.

Whatever course is adopted, in the ECC it is vital that the documentation (or Works Information in ECC terminology) states clearly what the *Contractor* is to design, otherwise the *Employer* will have to pay the additional costs for that design as a compensation event.

1.3.4 Application across different engineering disciplines

While the ECC originates from the Institution of Civil Engineers, it has been designed to be used on projects containing mechanical, electrical, civil or building elements, as well as on chemical process plants. Most contracts now involve an element of work from outside the main discipline, in some cases substantially so. For example, 50% of the cost of a building can sometimes be found in the mechanical and electrical services. A project in the heavy industrial engineering sector may well involve substantial civils work for the foundations and building work to house the facility, as well as computerised control systems. Whether the management of the interfaces between different works packages is done by the Employer or passed down to a main Contractor who then subcontracts the various packages, the integration and control is not helped by having different, and often incompatible, conditions of contract for each discipline. To accommodate the multi-disciplinary nature of the modern construction industry the ECC

- omits technical information, including detailed testing and commissioning requirements. Instead, it gives an outline framework for testing and quality procedures. The detail will then be included in the Works Information part of the contract documentation. It has been argued by some that one of the reasons the ECC is so short compared with traditional conditions of contract is that it excludes a lot of technical information which other conditions contain e.g. testing requirements. The counter argument is that these requirements are project-specific. To have in-depth testing requirements in the conditions of contract means that, in many cases, they are inappropriate to the technology involved. This applies even more so when the conditions of contract are intended to be used across a whole range of disciplines.

- uses some different terminology from that used in some sectors of the industry. For instance, what is known as construction plant and temporary works in the civil and building sectors are covered by the contractual definition of Equipment (clause 11.2 (11)). Plant and Materials are items included in the *works* (clause 11.2 (10)) i.e. permanent works in traditional civil engineering terminology. This can cause some initial confusion until people are familiar with the terminology .

The ECC has been used successfully on contracts in the civil engineering, building, power and water industries. However, one of the conclusions of the research was that in building contracts that are substantially designed at tender, the use of the ECC may be less appropriate due to the high number of small value changes which are sometimes introduced and the rigour with which time and cost effects of a compensation event are calculated in the ECC. This can be very time consuming. Counter to the research finding with respect to the use of *activity schedules* and *bills of quantities* (section 1.3.1.1.), it may be more appropriate to use Option B or D in these circumstances, as a bill rate can easily and quickly be used as a basis for the assessment of additional costs under clause 63.9. Of course, if an Employer knows what he wants and the building is well designed then there should not be too many changes.

1.3.5 International use

The NEC was written for international use. As such it does not attempt to paraphrase existing law and attempts to use simple language understandable to those whose first language is not English. The secondary options also contain clauses which might be suitable for contracts let in the developing world e.g. Option K: multiple currencies and Option N: price adjustment for inflation.

Secondary options which may only be selected for work in the United Kingdom are

- Option U: The Construction (Design and Management) Regulations 1994, which can be selected to compensate the *Contractor* if an event affecting safety occurs which an experienced contractor could not reasonably be expected to have foreseen.
- Option Y: The Housing Grants, Construction and Regeneration Act (1996) was issued as an addendum in 1998 as the payment and adjudication core clauses of the ECC do not comply with the Act. Either the Parties have to draft their own clauses, as some *Employers* have, or specify this option otherwise parts of 'the Scheme for Construction Contracts' will apply by default.

Some of the countries in which the NEC/ECC have been used include:

- Thailand, on a £67.5 million, 40 floor hotel and 38 floor residential development.
- Hong Kong, where it was used by the then Royal Hong Kong Jockey Club, a charitable organisation which uses betting receipts to fund racecourse and other leisure developments. Following the trial use on two projects worth approximately £3 million, it was then used on two multi-disciplinary projects worth £23 and £64 million.
- South Africa, where it has been used extensively by ESKOM, the world's seventh largest power generating company, which now lets virtually all of its engineering and construction projects

under the ECC or a prototype Short Form. Following their example, other companies in South Africa have adopted it.

Additionally, it is understood that following successful experiences in South Africa, a number of German contractors have now introduced its use into Germany.

The research from which this guide is derived primarily investigated contracts let in the UK. However, some comments were received from individuals involved in contracts abroad when they visited the UK. Favourable comments on the ECCs use of plain English included

- a *Contractor's* project director from Hong Kong, reporting how, for the first time in his experience, engineers from different countries, none of whose first language was English, would discuss the meaning of conditions of contract rather than leave it to the English quantity surveyors
- how the relative ease with which it can be understood by a comparatively uneducated work-force was one of the reasons behind its adoption and subsequent extensive use in South Africa.

1.3.6 Conclusion on flexibility

The ECC offers considerable flexibility in the range of contract strategies and engineering disciplines for which it can be used. This flexibility has been used in practice. A survey by the Institution of Civil Engineers, conducted in mid-1997, found that the most commonly used option was Option A (40%), followed by Option B (24%), Option C (22%), Option F (6%) and Options D and E (4% each). The greater proportion of contracts let under Option A compared with Option B reflect the advantages in practice of activity schedules over bills of quantities. As target cost contracts become more popular — for instance, over a half a billion pounds worth of contracts have already been let on the Channel Tunnel Rail Link — the proportion of contracts let under Option C should also increase. As previously stated it has successfully been used in the civil, building, water and power industries. Because of the volume and type of use in

South Africa, it has almost certainly been used more in the power industry than in any other sector.

1.4 OVERVIEW OF THE NEC ENGINEERING AND CONSTRUCTION CONTRACT

The purpose of this overview is to give a reader new to the ECC a rapid understanding of the terminology used, of the principal clauses and how the contract fits together. It is not a legal interpretation of the contract. The ECC uses some terminology which is different from traditional construction conditions of contract. This is partly to move away from old terminology with emotive connotations e.g. compensation events replace claims and variations, partly because of the multi-disciplinary application of the contract and partly to stimulate better project management.

In giving this overview, the author acknowledges that, to an extent, it simplifies or glosses over the detail. It is preferable that the reader reads this section with the ECC contract open beside him. If desired, the detail can be investigated, with help of the ECC guidance notes, flow charts and/or legal commentaries.

1.4.1 Contract data and defined terms

The <u>Contract Data</u> is contract-specific data and can be found at the back of the contract. Part I is filled out by the *Employer* prior to putting the contract out to tender and Part II is returned by the *Contractor* with his tender. It can be likened to Appendices to the Form of Contract/Tender in other standard forms, although as one *Project Manager* commented, 'it is a very useful checklist of issues which you should consider before putting a contract out to tender, and if you haven't thought about them by then, then you should do'. Information in the Contract Data is brought into the contract either by the ECC expressly stating that the information is in the Contract Data or by the use of *italics* (clause 11.1). Where italics are used, the reader should be able to substitute in the specific name, time scale, date or number (as appropriate) stated in the Contract Data. This convention is followed in this book when mentioning a party or term in a context specific to the ECC.

Defined terms have Capital Initials (clause 11.1) and can be found in clause 11.2. Therefore, whenever the reader comes across a term with capital letters he can refer to clause 11.2 to find out its contractual meaning. Further explanation of some of these terms is given below. Where the ECC uses capitals, then so does this book.

1.4.2 Parties and participants in the contract

The Parties to the contract are the *Employer* and *Contractor* (clause 11.2 (1)). Other participants mentioned in the contract are the *Project Manager* and the *Supervisor*. There is only one general statement of how these individuals act: they 'shall act as stated in this contract and in a spirit of mutual trust and co-operation' (clause 10.1). How they act in specific circumstances and the basis for their actions are defined in the individual clauses of the contract.

The *Employer's* interests are represented by the *Project Manager* who manages the contract on the *Employer's* behalf. The author would emphasise the word 'manage' because the ECC places a much greater onus on the *Project Manager* to manage than do traditional conditions of contract. This implies that

- the person selected should be more management orientated than technical orientated, although it is desirable that he has an appreciation of the technical aspects
- he must be delegated sufficient powers to take the actions and decisions required of him within the time scales of the contract
- the *Project Manager* knows and understands the business drivers behind the project, so that he can make decisions which best reflect the *Employer's* objectives.

The *Supervisor* is responsible for ensuring that the *Contractor* satisfies the quality standards stated in the specification or Works

Information in ECC terminology. The role has been described as somewhere between the traditional Architect/Resident Engineer/ Employer's Representative role and the Clerk of Works/Inspector's role. It has, in some cases, been seen as a demotion for the former roles. This can partly be counteracted by delegating some of the day-to-day duties of the *Project Manager* to the *Supervisor*.

Designers and architects are not mentioned in the ECC. Therefore, any *Employer* designer-originated design changes have to come through the *Project Manager*. This is so that the *Project Manager* can exercise control over the extent of changes issued by the designers. This does not stop works (sub)contractors and designers talking in order to determine the best technical solution, but does mean that the *Project Manager* can evaluate the effects of the proposed technical solution on time and cost before notifying the *Contractor* to proceed with the work. Where the *Contractor* is subcontracting some or all of his design under the Professional Services Contract, it is suggested that a person in the contractor organisation acts a buffer to the designers in a similar manner to that of the *Project Manager* in the ECC.

The *Adjudicator* is a third party who is called upon to decide on any dispute between the parties that cannot be settled by themselves. Adjudication is designed to be a relatively quick, inexpensive and less procedural way of settling disputes compared with arbitration or litigation. The Adjudicator's costs are paid jointly by the parties. As a result of the Housing Grants, Construction and Regeneration Act (1996), it is now compulsory to have an Adjudicator on virtually every construction project let in England, Wales and Northern Ireland. The Institution of Civil Engineers have issued an addendum to the ECC, Secondary Option Y(UK)2, so that it complies with the Act. Both the unamended and amended clauses have specified time scales once a dispute is notified. Under the unamended clauses, there is a time scale for the submission of the dispute, whereas, under the amended clauses (due to the requirements of the Act), a dispute can be referred 'at any time' to the *Adjudicator* (Option Y(UK)2.5 clause 90.5) (see section 3.5.5 for more detailed comments).

A Subcontractor is defined in clause 11.2 (9). Clause 26 refers to subcontracting and clause 26.1 makes it clear that the main contract applies as if the Subcontractors employees and resources are the main *Contractors*.

1.4.3 Some other defined terms

The Works Information and Site Information (clauses 11.2 (5) and (6)), together effectively form the specification and drawings in the traditional sense of the word. Project management is sometimes described as the management of change and the Site Information describes the starting point for that change, while the Works Information describes the end point of change and any constraints on how the *Contractor* is to achieve this end point. The drawing and documents that make up the Works and Site Information are referenced in the Contract Data. The Works Information can be changed by an instruction of the *Project Manager*, in which case it becomes a compensation event, except in two circumstances (clause 60.1 (1)). If unexpected physical conditions are encountered which satisfy the criteria in clauses 60.1 (12) and 60.2, then a compensation event results.

The Site (clause 11.2 (7)) is the area within the *boundaries of the site* as identified in the Contract Data by the *Employer* for use by the *Contractor* to Provide the Works.

The Working Areas (clause 11.2 (8)) are the Site and any additional areas identified by the *Contractor* in the Contract Data Part II which are needed to Provide the Works. The *Contractor* can propose additions to the Working Areas during the contract, but if the *Project Manager* rejects his submission for reasons not stated in clause 15.1, then it is a compensation event under clause 60.1(9).

'Plant and Materials are items intended to be included in the *works*' (clause 11.2 (10)), while Equipment (clause 11.2 (11)) is, in conventional building and civil engineering terms, construction plant and includes 'temporary works'. The reason for the change is because of the multi-disciplinary application of the ECC. For instance, in the heavy engineering sectors, such as the power and process sectors, plant is machinery that is delivered to the Site, bolted in and connected up e.g. generators and turbines.

Under the ECC, to be contractually valid, all <u>communications</u> have to be in a form which can be 'read, copied or recorded' (clause 13.1). For most purposes, this is in writing, but it could be in electronic format. Unless stated elsewhere in the contract — which it is for many procedures — all contractual communications have to be responded to within the *period for reply* (clause 13.3) , which is stated by the *Employer* in the Contract Data Part I. The most appropriate *period for reply* will vary between types of contract, e.g. on a design and build contract, where the *Project Manager* has to accept the *Contractor's* design compared with a traditional construction only contract, or it could be varied for different types of response. Failure by the *Project Manager* or *Supervisor* to respond within the periods required by the contract is a compensation event under clause 60.1.

1.4.4 Terminology for time

<u>Completion</u> (clause 11.2 (13)) is the equivalent of practical or substantial completion in traditional conditions of contract. However, it is more tightly defined in the ECC conditions. The first bullet point of clause 11.2 (13) states that the *Contractor* has to do 'all the work which the Works Information states he is to do'. Therefore, if some operations, e.g. landscaping on a road contract, do not have to be completed for the *Contractor* to achieve Completion, the Works Information should state this. The second bullet point states that the *Contractor* has to correct notified Defects which prevent the *Employer* from using the *works* i.e. the works have to be fit for purpose. It is the *Project Manager* who certifies Completion under clause 30.2.

The <u>Completion Date</u> is the date by which the *Contractor* has to achieve Completion. If the secondary option for delay damages is selected (Option R) and the *Contractor* fails to achieve Completion by the Completion Date, then the *Contractor* will have damages deducted at the rate prescribed in the Contract Data Part I. The original Completion Date is stated in the Contract Data and may be changed as a consequence of compensation events. The relevant clause is 63.3. If the *Project Manager*, acting on the *Employer's* behalf, wishes to bring forward the Completion Date, then the acceleration procedures in clause 36 are followed.

Clause 11.2 (14) states 'The <u>Accepted Programme</u> is the programme identified in the Contract Data or is the latest programme accepted by the *Project Manager*. The latest programme accepted by the *Project Manager* supersedes previous Accepted Programmes'. Revised programmes are submitted at intervals no longer than that stated in the Contract Data Part I. In the research sample, none of the 14 programmes submitted with the tender and referenced in Contract Data were incorporated into the contract, so none became the Accepted Programme, until they had been further refined once the contract was signed.

What the first programme has to show is stated in clause 31.2 and this includes method statements and resources for each operation, as well as float and time risk allowances (the difference between best productivity and average productivity). Until a programme is submitted which shows the information required by the contract, a quarter of the Price for Work Done to Date is retained from amounts due to the *Contractor* (clause 50.3). Once such a programme has been submitted, this sanction cannot be applied. To be accepted the programme has to satisfy the criteria stated in clause 31.3. Any revised programme has to show the information in clauses 31.2 and 32.1 and to be accepted has to again satisfy the criteria stated in clause 31.3. In addition to the sanction in clause 50.3 for a programme which does not contain the information required, it is mandatory for the *Project Manager* to assess compensation events if various criteria for the programme are not satisfied (clauses 64.1 and 64.2). On the basis that the *Contractor* knows more about the change in resources etc. due to a compensation event than the *Project Manager*, this is likely to result in a less favourable assessment of any additional time and money to which the *Contractor* is entitled.

The reason for incorporating these contractual incentives in the ECC is that the Accepted Programme is the base document from which both the time and cost effects of compensation events are assessed. Thus if a compensation event occurs resulting in a change in method, then the resulting changes in resources are compared with those in the current Accepted Programme. Providing these resources are in the Schedule of Cost Components, then costs are assigned to these changed resources. Any change to the Completion Date is again evaluated by comparison with the latest Accepted Programme.

The programme is a document vital to the administration and management of the contract and, as such, it is worthwhile

- for the *Contractor* to spend time developing the programme so that the *Project Manager* can understand where his costs come from and to avoid the sanctions

- for the *Project Manager* to spend time understanding the *Contractor's* programme, ensuring that it both satisfies the requirements of the contract and does not commit him, the *Employer* or Others to a deadline that they cannot fulfil e.g. delivery to Site of something to be incorporated into the *works*. If the *Project Manager* is unhappy with the programme, he should not be afraid to exercise the powers available to him.

1.4.5 *Terminology for quality*

Clause 11.2 (15) describes what a <u>Defect</u> is.

The <u>*defects date*</u> is defined in the Contract Data Part I as a period of weeks after Completion of the whole of the *works* and is equivalent to a maintenance period. Until the *defects date*, the *Supervisor* notifies the *Contractor* of any Defects which he finds and vice versa (clause 42.2).

If notified on or before Completion — and providing the Defect does not prevent the *Employer* from using the *works* and thus affect Completion — the *Contractor* has, from the time of Completion, the <u>*defects correction period*</u> (stated in the Contract Data Part I) to correct any notified Defects. For any Defects notified in between Completion and the *defects date*, from the time of the notification, the *Contractor* has the <u>*defects correction period*</u> to correct any Defects (clause 43.1).

The <u>Defects Certificate</u> is a certificate issued by the *Supervisor* which states that there are no Defects or is a list of Defects which the

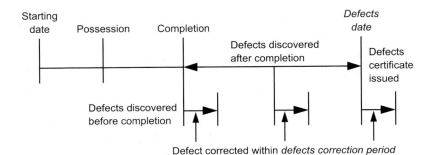

Fig. 2. Illustration of time scales for correction of defects

Contractor has not corrected (clause 11.2 (16)). It is issued by the *Supervisor* at 'at the later of the *defects date* and the end of the last *defect correction period*' (clause 43.2). Fig. 2 illustrates these concepts.

Clauses 43.3, 44 and 45 give various options to the *Project Manager* if the *Contractor* does not correct Defects within the *defect correction period*.

1.4.6 Terminology for payment

The <u>Schedule of Cost Components</u> is a generic list of resources which may be used to Provide the Works. It has the following headings: People, Plant and Materials, Equipment, Charges (which would commonly be called Preliminaries in civil engineering or building), off-site Manufacture and Fabrication, off-site Design, and Insurances. It is found at the back of the contract and is split into what shall be referred to as the normal Schedule of Cost Components (or normal Schedule) and the Shorter Schedule of Cost Components (or Shorter Schedule). The Shorter Schedule is simplified and is intended to be used to assess the financial effects of relatively minor straightforward compensation events. Both Schedules contain round-up percentages to avoid excessive costs in determining for minutiae e.g. the cost of hand tools. Under the:

40

- <u>Priced Options (A and B)</u>, the Schedules are used for assessing compensation events. If the *Contractor* is to be paid for a compensation event, then the change in resources is determined using the method statements and resources forming part of the Accepted Programme. For the *Contractor* to be paid more (or less), the changed resource has to be listed in the Schedule of Cost Components and the change in the *Contractor's* Actual Costs are worked out in accordance with the Schedule.

- <u>Target Options (C and D)</u> and the <u>Cost Reimbursable Option (E)</u>, the *Contractor* is reimbursed any costs which are listed in the normal Schedule of Cost Components. If a compensation event occurs, then the change to the target under the target contracts or estimate of final cost under the cost reimbursable contract (both referred to as the Prices in ECC terminology — see below) is worked out in the same way as for the priced options (see section 1.3.1.3 for a brief explanation of how target cost contracts work).

- <u>Management Option (F)</u>, the Schedule of Cost Components is not mentioned as the management *Contractor* will do very little, if any, of the physical work. Assuming the works packages are let under Options A to E of the NEC Engineering and Construction Subcontract, then the Schedule of Cost Components will be used in the same way as in the ECC.

<u>Actual Cost</u> is the term used in the main options clauses (except Option F) to reference the Schedule of Cost Components.

- Under the <u>Priced Options (A and B)</u>, 'Actual Cost is the cost of the components in the Schedule of Cost Components whether work is subcontracted or not excluding the cost of preparing quotations for compensation events' (clause 11.2 (28)).

- Under the <u>Target Options (C and D)</u> and the <u>Cost Reimbursable Option (E)</u>, 'Actual Cost is the amount of payments due to Subcontractors for work which is subcontracted and the cost of the components in the Schedule of Cost Components for work which is not subcontracted, less any Disallowed Cost' (clause 11.2 (27)).

41

- Under the Management Contract Option (F), 'Actual Cost is the amount of payments due to Subcontractors for work which the *Contractor* is required to subcontract, less any Disallowed Cost' (clause 11.2 (26)). It does not reference the Schedule of Cost Components.

The definition of Disallowed Cost varies between the main options. No definition exists for the Priced Options (A and B). Clause 11.2 (30) applies to the Target Options (C and D) and Cost Reimbursable Option (E), while 11.2 (29) applies to the Management Contract Option (F). Essentially, Disallowed Cost results from the *Contractor* not complying with various provisions of the contract or from not using the resources properly on the particular contract.

Under all options, 'the Fee is the amount calculated by applying the *fee percentage* to the amount of Actual Cost' (clause 11.2 (17)). The *fee percentage* is tendered by the *Contractor* in the Contract Data Part II. For compensation events, the *fee percentage* is applied to the change in Actual Costs (clause 63.1) of the *Contractor* to adjust the Prices. For the Options C to F, it is also applied to the Actual Costs spent (Options C, D and E) or accepted for payment (Option F) by the *Contractor* i.e. the *Contractor* is paid on a cost plus percentage fee basis.

Various definitions exist for the Prices and the Price for Work Done to Date depending on which main options are used.

The Prices
- Under all options, the initial Prices represent the initial estimate of what it will cost the *Employer* for the *Contractor* to do the work.
- Under the Priced Options (A and B), the Prices are tendered by or agreed in negotiation with the *Contractor* and are either the sum of
  ○ under Option A, the individual prices against each of the ac-tivities in the *activity schedule*, or
  ○ under Option B, the lump sums and the sum of rates times quantities.

If there are no compensation events, the Prices are the amount the *Contractor* will receive for providing the *works*. As the contract progresses some compensation events will inevitably occur and the Prices will be changed to reflect the cost effect of these compensation events.

- Under the Target Cost Options (C and D), the total of the Prices is the target. It is either tendered by or agreed in negotiation with the *Contractor* and is either the sum of
  - under Option C, the individual prices against each of the activities in the *activity schedule*, or
  - under Option D, the lump sums and the sum of rates times quantities.

Once again, as the contract progresses some compensation events will inevitably occur and the Prices will be changed to reflect the cost effect of these compensation events. However, the Prices are the target and as such are the fulcrum around which the incentive mechanism operates. It is not what the *Contractor* is paid.

- Under the Cost Reimbursable and Management Options (E and F), the Prices are defined as 'the Actual Cost plus the Fee' with Fee being a percentage of Actual Cost. However, while the Prices are modified by compensation events, their only function is as an estimate of the final monetary sum that will be paid to the *Contractor*.

Under all options, the principal clause governing the evaluation of the cost effects of compensation events is clause 63.1. It means that the change in the Prices, due to the compensation event, is effectively equal to the change in Actual Costs or forecast Actual Costs and the resulting Fee. Therefore to work out the change in Actual Costs, it is necessary to first evaluate the Actual Cost of the original work item, then the Actual Cost of the revised work item, and then the subtraction of one from the other gives the change in Actual Costs to which the *fee percentage* is applied. In practice, some short cuts can be taken by agreement. Under the *bill of quantities* Options (B and D), 'if the *Project Manager* and the *Contractor* agree, rates and lump sums in the *bill of quantities* may be used as a basis for assessment instead of Actual Cost and the resulting Fee' (clause 63.9).

The Price for Work Done to Date.

- Under the Priced Options (A and B), the Price for Work Done to Date is the total of the Prices, at any point in the contract, for
  - each group of completed activities or complete activity (clause 11.2 (24) in Option A), or
  - the quantity multiplied by the rate in the *bill of quantities* plus a proportion of each lump sum (clause 11.2 (25) in Option B) which are without Defects that delay or are covered by immediately following work.
- Under the Target Cost Options (C and D) and the Cost Reimbursable Option (E), 'the Price for Work Done to Date is the Actual Cost which the *Contractor* has paid plus the Fee' (clause 11.2 (23)) i.e. the *Contractor* has to have paid it out in order to be reimbursed, thus encouraging rapid payment down the contractual chain. It should be noted that, if the final Price for Work Done to Date exceeds the final total of the Prices, then the *Contractor's* share of the overrun will be paid back to the *Employer* following Completion. If the final Price for Work Done to Date is less than the final total of the Prices, then the *Contractor* will be paid his share of any saving by the *Employer* following Completion.
- Under the Management Contract (Option F), 'the Price for Work Done to Date is the Actual Cost which the *Contractor* has accepted for payment plus the Fee'. The *Contractor* is therefore paid in advance. The rationale is that the *Contractor* is doing little if any of the physical work himself, so it is unreasonable to expect him to finance it.

1.4.7 Early warning and the compensation event procedure

The Early Warning (clause 16) is a procedure whereby the *Project Manager* and *Contractor* have to notify each other of any matter which may increase the Prices, delay Completion or impair the performance of the *works* in use. The stimulus on the *Project Manager* to early warn is that the project is likely to suffer if he does not. The stimulus on the *Contractor* is that if the early warning subsequently becomes or results in a compensation event (and not all necessarily will), then 'the event is assessed as if the *Contractor* has given an early warning' (clause 63.4). The absence of an early warning by the *Contractor* may therefore lead to loss of compensation. All *Contractors* in the research sample early warned as a matter of policy.

Having issued an early warning notification, either may instruct the other to attend an early warning meeting — which need not be a formal affair — where they consider how best to deal with the matter. The *Project Manager* records the proposals considered and gives a copy to the *Contractor*.

Compensation events are a list of events for which the *Contractor* may be entitled to time and monetary compensation. They are listed in clause 60.1. (plus an additional three in the *bill of quantities* Options B and D (clauses 60.4 to 60.6)). The 'may be' is because the compensation event is the trigger, but the *Contractor* still has to justify changes in the Completion Date and his Actual Costs for him to obtain additional time and money.

The majority of compensation events are for events over which the *Employer*, *Project Manager* or *Supervisor* have full or predominant control. The exceptions, and of particular interest, are clauses 60.1 (12) and 60.1 (13).

- The *Contractor* 'encounters physical conditions . . . which an experienced contractor would have judged . . . to have such a small chance of occurring that it would have been unreasonable for him to have allowed for them'. This differs from the reasonable foreseeability test found in more traditional construction contracts. Further clarification to this clause is given in clause 60.2. The intended effect is to put a greater onus on the *Employer* to supply more information at tender stage on the Site conditions. A thorough site investigation reduces risk generally and if this information is given to the *Contractor*, then a greater proportion of this reduced risk is transferred to the *Contractor*.

- The *weather measurements* recorded occur on average less frequently than once in ten years, with the one in ten year weather measurements being referred to as the *weather data*. This is a much more clear cut test compared with the subjective 'exceptional(ly) adverse weather' criteria of other contracts.

The procedures for notifying, quoting for, assessing and implementing compensation events are described in clauses 61 to 65. The same procedure applies whichever compensation event occurs and under whichever main option has been chosen. The *Contractor* is always entitled to profit (in the form of the tendered *fee* percentage applied to the change in his Actual Costs arising from a compensation event). The maximum time scales are illustrated in Fig. 3.

Starting at the top left side, the *Contractor's* notification of a compensation event is not valid if it is more than two weeks since he became aware of the compensation event (clause 61.3). The intention of the authors of the ECC is to force the *Contractor* to notify compensation events promptly, otherwise any entitlement to additional time and money is lost. The *Project Manager* has one week to respond and will either instruct the *Contractor* to submit a quotation or not to submit for one of the stated reasons (clause 61.4).

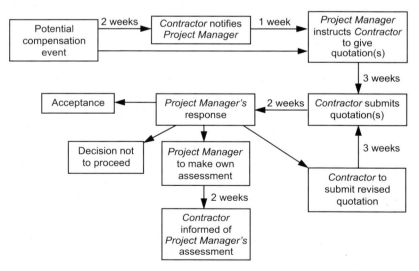

Fig. 3. Maximum time scales for responses for compensation events

There is no time bar on the *Project Manager* informing the *Contractor* of a compensation event and asking him for a quotation.

Having asked for a quotation, the *Contractor* has a maximum of three weeks to supply one — unless a longer period is agreed (clause 61.4) — otherwise the *Project Manager* assesses the compensation event (clause 64.1). If this is the case, then from the time when the need for the *Project Manager's* assessment becomes apparent, he has the same period as the *Contractor* to supply the quotation (clause 64.3).

On receiving the *Contractor's* quotation, the *Project Manager* has a maximum of two weeks — unless an extended period is agreed — either to

- accept it
- ask for a re-submission, stating his reasons, in which case the *Contractor* has a further three weeks to re-submit it
- decide not to proceed with the compensation event, assuming it is being assessed prior to the work proceeding, or
- notify the *Contractor* that he will be making his own assessment, in which case the *Project Manager* has up to three weeks to make that assessment from the time of the notification.

If the *Project Manager* makes an assessment and the *Contractor* disagrees, then the *Contractor* can refer the matter to Adjudication. It is therefore always preferable that the *Contractor* prepares the quotation and the *Project Manager* accepts it, even after revision.

When a compensation event occurs, the change to the Completion Date is assessed following the rule set out in clause 63.3. (For the cost effects see under Prices earlier in this section). Clause 63.3 means that the Completion Date can only be changed to a later date or kept where it is due to a compensation event, and it is put back by the same amount of time that planned Completion is delayed compared to the current Accepted Programme. This has several implications, namely

- no compensation event can result in an earlier Completion Date. Acceleration in the ECC means bringing the Completion Date forward, and this has to be done through the acceleration provisions (clause 36). If a compensation event occurs which would delay the Completion Date, the *Project Manager* can ask the *Contractor* to produce a quotation, under the compensation event procedure, for the work to be speeded up so that the existing Completion Date is achieved, but not bettered.

- the *Contractor* will want to show as little free float as possible in his Accepted Programme, i.e. all operations are close to or on the critical path, so that any compensation event puts back Completion and hence the Completion Date. This is one of the reasons it is important for the *Project Manager* to spend time evaluating the *Contractor's* programme submissions before accepting them.

1.5 STIMULUS TO GOOD MANAGEMENT

The ECC's third aim is the stimulus to good management. Because of the all embracing scope of 'management', in this brief overview consideration is only given to project management relating to the construction phase. While achievement of 'good management' is an objective both of the ECC and presumably of the companies that contract under it, it is an enabling objective in that 'good management' should lead to a higher likelihood of the project and company objectives being fulfilled.

Therefore, before looking at what constitutes good management and how conditions of contract can contribute to its achievement, it is perhaps worthwhile asking what the 'stimuli' to good management are, i.e. what Employer's and Contractor's objectives are. The reason for considering this is so that both parties understand what the other wants from a contract, so that potential users of the ECC can appreciate how, by its procedures and sanctions, it aims to create the right environment for good project management, including co-operation, to flourish. Several contracts in the research sample failed to fully achieve their objectives because the participants initially failed to understand how by working within the principles, spirit and words of the ECC, rather than against them or ignoring them, they could increase the likelihood of achieving their own individual objectives.

1.5.1 *Stimulus to the* Contractor

The Contractor or Subcontractor are often seen as purely profit maximisation organisations. This is an over-simplification. Contractors

- in the short term, need a positive cash flow to pay their bills. If expenditure exceeds income over a sustained period of time then a company will not continue operating. The more positive cash flow is, the more profit a company makes, either through not paying interest or being paid interest. Particularly in the civil engineering and building sectors where profit margins are frequently less than a few percent, a short delay in payment can have serious effects on profit margin and a huge effect on return on investment. Virtually all of the *Contractors* interviewed in the research commented on how their cash flow was more positive compared with contracts let under traditional forms of contract.

- wish to produce a profit on any contract they enter into. Unsurprisingly, they prefer profit levels from a contract to be predictable compared to fluctuating and unpredictable. For any business, not knowing when or how much you will be paid for completed work does not aid the running of a business, yet it would appear to be almost accepted practice in much of the construction industry. A few contractors, within the research sample, increased their expected profit on turnover by between 3 and 4%. A commonly expressed view by *Contractors* was that there was more certainty under the ECC that a reasonable profit would be achieved, provided they complied with the requirements of the contract. Representatives of both the *Employers* and *Contractors* thought that the potential to make 'silly money' was not within the ECC.

- may want a satisfied Employer, so that they win repeat order or referred business. The 'may' depends on the nature of the Employer. For instance, if the next contract will be awarded on lowest cost criteria whatever the Contractor's performance on the previous one or if the Employer is unlikely to place another contract, then this motive may be subjugated in order to pursue the first two.

1.5.2 *Stimulus to the* Employer

A project has three prime objectives: time, cost and quality. To improve the performance of one can lead to a decrease in the others. For example, to decrease the time scale of a project, it will generally be necessary to increase expenditure and vice versa. However, within each of these objectives there are also some trade-offs, which are now briefly examined.

- *Quality* A company, in commissioning a project, is doing so to satisfy a perceived need or function. It is argued, therefore that an Employer's prime objective is to have an asset that performs the function identified for it i.e. it is 'fit for purpose'. It is not worth paying, for example, £999 for an asset that does not perform the function required, when you could pay £1000 for one that does. As a project progresses into the construction phase, Employers inevitably wish to introduce some changes to ensure or increase functionality or performance, so some flexibility is often required. Any change has effects on time and cost, so there is a need for a rational, consistent and accepted method to evaluate these effects.
- *Cost* There is a potential trade-off between certainty of cost and potential minimum cost. For instance, if the Employer is liable for the majority of risks that may eventuate, the risk premium in the tender will be low, resulting in a low tender. If none of the risks occur he will not pay anything additional to the tendered price, but if they do occur then he may pay a great deal more. If, however, he allocates the risks to the Contractor, then he will be charged a greater premium for them and the tender will be higher, but the Employer will have greater certainty.
- *Time* To a lesser extent, what applies to cost also applies to time.

What comes out of these three brief glimpses is that Employers will generally want an element of certainty over the time, cost and quality parameters when they sanction a project and let an individual contract. To gain certainty, they have to firstly have effective monitoring procedures for time, cost and quality parameters — so that they have knowledge of when a project or contract is deviating from the expected parameters — and secondly they have to be able to exercise control in order to bring the project back into the planned parameters. Knowledge of where a contract is heading, in terms of time and cost, and the ability to influence it leads to greater certainty. These were the most often cited advantages of using the ECC by *Employers* and their representatives.

However, this is not the whole story. A number of studies have found little correlation between satisfaction expressed by Employers and project performance expressed in absolute terms of cost and time. Other factors, such as the smoothness and efficiency with which their needs are fulfilled by the industry, play a large part in their judgement of the level of success. In the authors' opinion, this equates to level of service and could include ease of working with, and agreeing issues with the Contractor and speed of settling the final account. Under the ECC, the final account was settled at the time of Completion on one contract subject to major changes. Often it was settled within a month and rarely took more than three months. Those that took longer than this did not display the majority of characteristics outlined in Part III. Minimum hassle also means that both parties can concentrate on their core businesses. For the Contractor, it is argued that this should be building the Employer a functional asset within time and cost parameters, and not devoting considerable time and overhead clawing back money through claims in order to make a profit. For an Employer, it is argued that this should not be spending time and money fighting these claims.

1.5.3 Good management

This section addresses the ways in which the procedures within the ECC aid effective project management of the contract. It assumes a basic level of knowledge about the ECC and explains things in ECC terminology. For those not familiar with ECC, it is suggested that section 1.4 is read prior to reading this section in order to gain this knowledge and understanding.

When conducting seminars on the ECC, the author often asks participants what factors increase the likelihood of the objectives of a project being achieved. Frequently, there is little response, presumably because people have not thought about these factors or are unaware of them. Below is a list of some factors which are likely to increase the likelihood of an engineering or construction project achieving its objectives

- clearly defined objectives
- quality personnel
- clear, unambiguous and complete information supplied to the Contractor
- minimal change introduced during the construction period
- appropriate contract strategy to align motivations. This was discussed in some detail in section 1.3, including the selection of the appropriate main and secondary options and level of *Contractor* design
- clear and appropriate definitions of roles and responsibilities
- proper and clear allocation of risk
- sufficient testing requirements to ensure fitness for purpose
- integration of actual progress and expenditure compared with planned progress and expenditure
- early identification of potential problems
- an effective, equitable and rapid procedure for evaluating the time and cost effect of changes
- options for dealing with the unexpected
- transparency and communication leading to co-operation between the parties
- an inexpensive and fair procedure for rapid resolution of disagreements.

The first four of these points are relatively independent of the type of contract used, but they and the other points are discussed briefly below.

Clearly defined objectives. It is a matter of common sense that to achieve the project objectives, you have to know what they are. It is therefore worthwhile spending time defining them, including any constraints, before rushing into the construction. For example, if the asset has to be fit for purpose, what is its purpose? What is the balance between cost (or time) certainty and the desire for minimum cost (or time)? From this flows a proper definition of the project from which flows a description of what is required and from whom.

Quality personnel. Ultimately, it is not conditions of contract that build things, but organisations which consist of individuals. If the people involved are not of sufficient quality, in terms of technical, managerial and people skills or have incompatible attitudes, then the process of construction will be adversely affected, which in turn will affect the likely outcome. Guidance on these attributes is given in section 3.1.3.

Clear, unambiguous and complete information supplied to the Contractor. In ECC terms, this means good quality Site and Works Information, so that the *Contractor* knows what he is to do to complete the contract and hence can price and programme the job properly. For guidance on the preparation of ECC documentation see section 3.1.1. In the longer term, the ECC has helped improve the quality of contract documentation. Major users found that the ECC more clearly highlights (not exaggerates) the time and costs of individual changes closer to the time that they occur. This compares to the common situation under traditional contracts, where the indirect costs of the changes are generally assessed together at the end of the contract as a claim for delay and disruption. Therefore, under the ECC, shortcomings in the documentation are more easily identified and the lessons learnt can be incorporated into the documentation for future contracts. It has made some experienced ECC Employers quite critical of their design teams' or consultants' performance!

Minimal change introduced during the construction period. A study in Canada, which drew data from over a billion dollars of work at today's prices from a number of construction sectors concluded that changes introduced after the contract is let, on average, cost approximately three times as much as if they were included in the original specification. Approximately, a third of this is on the direct costs, a third is spent on the prolongation element i.e. the additional time on sites and a third on the loss of productivity/disruption caused by the change.[*] The implication is that if those managing a project wish to increase the likelihood of it meeting its time, cost and performance objectives, then they need to have strict change control procedures and only allow changes, whether in scope or design, which are necessary for the project to achieve its function or performance objective.

Clear and appropriate definitions of roles and responsibilities are important so that participants know what function they are expected to perform within the contract team. The ECC has divided the traditional role of the Engineer or Architect into four separate roles: the designer, the *Project Manager*, the *Supervisor* and the *Adjudicator* (section 1.4.2). The intention is that each individual can specialise in his particular role, without conflicts of interest between roles. For example, in traditional construction contracts, the Resident Engineer is required to make an impartial judgement over a previous decision of his, say on the detail of a design, when that design may have been initially done by him or his company. The research found that roles and responsibilities were well defined in the ECC with few, if any, gaps or overlaps in responsibility.

Proper and clear allocation of risk. Proper allocation generally means that the party best able to minimise the likelihood of the risk occurring and to bear it is allocated the risk. Clear allocation means that there is little or no argument over financial ownership of the problem, and therefore who should take actions to prevent it

---

[*] Revay S. G. (1992). Can construction claims be avoided? In Fenn P. and Gameson R. (eds), *Construction conflict and resolution.* E & FN Spon.

occurring or minimise its impact if it does. Apart from the selection of the main and secondary options, risks allocated to the *Employer* are clearly listed as compensation events (clause 60.1). Because they are listed in one place (with the same assessment procedure for all of them), *Employers* have found it easier to delete or add a compensation event depending on the project circumstances. The research found that the definitions of *Employer's* risks are more clear cut than under traditional forms of contract. The main advantage of this is that contract participants spent less time arguing over whose risk something is. Consequently, the party whose risk it is can devote their efforts to managing the risk, rather than trying to avoid liability for it. The other party, knowing that it is not their risk, can contribute to the management of the risk without fear of admitting liability.

Sufficient testing requirements to ensure fitness for purpose. The ECC gives an outline framework for testing, which should be developed in the Works Information, so that it is specific and appropriate for contract strategy e.g. performance specification or pre-designed and the technology involved in the project. This helps ensure that the final product meets its quality parameters, but does require more specific thought by those putting together the documentation. If the work done fails to meet the quality parameters i.e. it is a Defect, then

- the procedure for correcting them is specified in clause 43
- the *Project Manager* has the option of trading quality off against time and cost by accepting the Defect in return for reduced Prices or an earlier Completion Date under clause 44
- the *Project Manager* has a sanction available to him, in clause 45, to encourage the *Contractor* to correct Defects within the *defects correction period.*

Integration of actual progress and expenditure compared with planned progress and expenditure aids monitoring. In the ECC

- what the programme is to show is stated in greater detail than in other traditional contracts (clause 31.2) and includes method statements and resources for each operation

- the programme is updated at regular intervals (clauses 32.1 and 32.2)
- sanctions exist to encourage the *Contractor* to show in the programmes the stated information (clause 50.3), to keep it up-to-date and for it to be practicable and realistic (clauses 64.1 and 64.2)
- if Option A, the priced contract with activity schedule, is used, then payment is directly linked to progress. If Option C, the target contract with activity schedule, is used the *Contractor* is reimbursed his costs plus Fee and expenditure can be compared to that anticipated in the *activity schedule* to determine trends in progress.

Many interviewees commented on the change in emphasis of the programme from a tool used to justify and extract claims at the end of the contract to a project management tool for the efficient and co-operative management of the work. Some *Contractors* have partly attributed their increased profit margin to this emphasis on programming, which as one commented, 'forces us to do what we should be doing in any case'.

Early identification of potential problems so that action can be taken to minimise their impact. The early warning procedure is designed to ensure both that problems are identified at the first opportunity and actions can be taken quickly to minimise their likelihood or impact. This is the intermediate step between risk management — identifying what can go wrong and developing strategies to minimise their impact — and monitoring where something has gone wrong and has already affected the works. There is a sanction on the *Contractor* should he not give an early warning (clause 63.4). The early warning procedure has proved extremely effective in operation. It has been described as 'the jewel in the NEC crown' and 'the starting point for co-operation'.

An effective, equitable and rapid procedure for evaluating changes. The core clauses of the ECC contains one procedure for evaluating both the time and cost effects of a compensation event (section 6 of the ECC). The compensation event procedure has clearly stated and tight time scales which are achievable in most circumstances (section 1.4.4). Sanctions put an onus on the *Contractor* to both notify the compensation event (clause 61.3) and submit a quotation for its effect within these time scales (clause 64.1). Once the quotation has been accepted by the *Project Manager* on the *Employer's* behalf, it cannot be re-opened (clause 65.2). The *Contractor* is compensated for the change in his Actual Costs and resulting Fee, with Actual Costs being drawn from the Schedule of Cost Components (clause 63.1). The intention is that it is a more rigorous and fairer method of evaluating the costs of changes. In practice, the compensation event procedure has caused some problems, partly due to unfamiliarity and the changes in practice it requires, but partly because it does not quite match how the *Contractor* incurs additional costs in certain circumstances (section 3.2.3). A key to the successful operation of the ECC is in the administration of the compensation event procedure (sections 3.5.3 and 3.5.4).

Options for dealing with the unexpected events. When an event occurs, there may well be more than one way of dealing with it. For compensation events, the *Project Manager* can ask for a number of quotations, based on different ways of dealing with a compensation event (clause 62.1), so that he can select the option which best matches his objectives. For instance, whether to implement a least time solution or least cost solution. This choice has been exercised in practice, although perhaps not as often it could have been.

Transparency and communication leading to co-operation between the parties. Participants to a contract will co-operate if they perceive it to be in their professional and commercial interests to do so. The alternative is confrontation and dispute. In 1992, it is estimated this cost the UK construction industry 7% of its turnover.[*] The

---

[*] Doyle N. (1993). Disputes under pressure. *New Builder*, 157, p. 12, 8th Jan.

traditional 'rules of the game' make it necessary for this money to be spent by Contractors to recover their costs in order to make a profit, and for Employers to fight these claims. However, it is an activity of the construction industry and their Employers which adds nothing to the value of the end product. The ECC aims to change the contractual rules and to stimulate co-operation with two inter-linked principles.

- *Transparency* The ECC's programming requirements require more information to be communicated, the early warning procedure requires each party to inform the other of any potential problem at the earliest opportunity and the Schedule of Cost Components provide an indisputable list of what the *Contractor* can include in his quotation for a compensation event.

- *Communication* The ECC requires people to communicate in a form which can be read, copied and recorded within laid down time scales, rather than 'in a reasonable time'. The effect of this, rather than making people write more letters, is generally to make people talk more and then to confirm and summarise what they have agreed in writing. The author is aware of one *Employer* who abandoned use of the ECC after one contract because of the administrative burden. At the opposite end of the spectrum, others have said that the paper work system set up meant that issues were resolved sooner and allowed them more time to concentrate on value adding or cost reducing activities such as programming. Guidance is given in section 3.4.3 on setting up an efficient communication system.

Rapid Dispute Resolution. The ECC has adjudication as its form of rapid dispute resolution. In the UK, as a result of the Housing Grants, Construction and Regeneration Act, adjudication is now compulsory on virtually all construction contracts. Other pre-adjudication dispute resolutions procedures can be incorporated if desired e.g. negotiation and conciliation/mediation or post-adjudication dispute procedures can be specified in the Contract Data as part of the tribunal, before moving onto the expense of arbitration or litigation procedures.

1.5.4 Conclusion on stimulus to good management

This section has outlined what the main stimuli to the parties of a contract are, so that each party gains not only a greater appreciation of other parties' objectives, but also to aid their understanding of what the ECC tries to achieve. It has also briefly outlined some of the components of good project management which affect the construction phase of a project, shown how they are promoted in the ECC through its procedures and given some feedback on the success of these procedures in aiding the achievement of the parties' objectives. Some users have stated that on the best run contracts, the factors identified in this section happen anyway. A question is 'why do they not always happen?'. An answer could be that the stimuli to make it in participants interests to do these things are not usually present. The ECC aims to provide these stimuli and the research has indicated that, by and large, it has been successful.* Part III addresses how readers can obtain the maximum benefits available from using the ECC.

However, conditions of contract are only part of the 'rules of the game'. Other factors include acceptance of the lowest tender regardless of whether the sum tendered is believed to be sufficient to cover the cost of work, poor quality specifications which give contractors opportunities to make claims etc. Other factors, such as appropriate contract strategy, use of lean construction principles and the various principles and techniques which come under the banner of partnering all help reduce cost and time and increase certainty and quality. In this respect, the ECC should not be seen as *the* answer — rather as part of the answer.

---

* Interestingly, having run an NEC contract, some Contractors have implemented the procedures learnt on NEC contracts on non-NEC. However, they have not passed the information that these procedures give them onto those representing the Employer, because it is not necessarily in their interests to do so.

1.6 CONCLUSION TO PART I

Part I has given readers substantial background information on the philosophy and ethos behind the ECC. The author has intended to give potential users an understanding of why the authors of the ECC chose clarity and simplicity; flexibility and stimulus to good management as the three key objectives. Greater guidance than that available in the current second edition has been given on the selection of the main and secondary options and other aspects of contract strategy. The important clauses and main procedures of the ECC were reviewed in order to give the reader an overview of how the contract fits together. Feedback from the research has been given on the ECC's effectiveness in delivering the aimed for benefits.

Given this information, readers should be able to

- make more informed decisions on whether they are willing to contract under the ECC
- make more informed decisions in the selection of the most appropriate contract strategy
- have an understanding of how the contract fits together in order to appreciate how the experiences in Part II and suggestions for best practice made in Part III can contribute both to the efficient and effective operation of the ECC and the achievement of their organisation's objectives.

Part II

Users' experiences

This section contains brief summaries from users who have represented *Employers, Contractors* and Subcontractors. The contributing individuals were asked to outline their initial reaction to the ECC, the differences in approach adopted prior to use compared with that under their normal conditions of contract, the differences they wish they had adopted with the benefit of hindsight and the advantages and disadvantages they have found in practice. Many, if not all, of the lessons learnt are discussed in greater detail in Part III. The comments also show that despite experiences on only one or two contracts, parties from all sides of the industry perceive the ECC as an improvement, to varying degrees, on the more traditional conditions of contract they are used to working under.

The Employer's View

Andrew Wrightson is a contracts officer for National Power plc. He was responsible for overseeing three trial contracts let under the first edition of the NEC in 1993 and is now responsible for contracts worth up to £85 million let under the ECC.

In the early 1990s, as a newly privatised utility, National Power were looking to rationalise the number of conditions of contract used to procure heavy engineering and construction works. We wanted a contract that allowed for Contractor design and that could be used across all our heavy engineering and construction projects, thereby allowing expertise developed on one contract to be used on another of a different technical discipline. We were about to start writing our own conditions when the consultative edition of the New Engineering Contract was brought to our attention. The reasons for our interest were its range of application within the same contractual framework and that it was written externally. It would therefore be perceived by Contractors as being more independent and fair than one written by ourselves. In addition, they would be able to obtain independent advice and training on it.

Following the first editions publication, we chose three contracts to trial it on: a coal dust handling contract, a civil engineering contract consisting predominantly of earth moving, and a coal weighing facility. These contracts were relatively low in value and risk. Having decided to go ahead with these contracts, we tried to really understand the detail of the contract by reading it carefully and attending internally and externally led seminars.

Partly as a result of this, we came to the conclusion that it was desirable to rewrite and rearrange our specifications — which were in need of an overhaul regardless of any change in the conditions of contract used. It seemed sensible to revise our standard specifications in a way which was both compatible with the NEC and followed its drafting philosophy.[*]

---

[*] For a more detailed account of the process and benefits, see section 3.1.1.

At the time of putting the individual contract out to tender, we invited the prospective Contractors in for a talk followed by a question and answer session. We would explain why we were using the NEC, give an overview of how it fitted together stressing that this was our interpretation only and advise them to seek external advice and training. On award, we would follow a similar procedure with both our and the Contractor's site team. This is because the people tendering are often different from the people running the contract and there is often a discontinuity of information. We would also discuss how we would run the job together. We continued with these procedures for the next two years until we felt that all the Contractors we work with on a regular basis were familiar with the main principles of the NEC.

In assessing tenders, we set, and still do, a notional contingency figure for compensation events to which we apply the tendered *fee percentage*. We then add this sum to the Prices for tender comparison purposes. We initially felt that further breaking down this contingency figure and then applying the relevant percentages tendered in the Contract Data Part II to people and Equipment was over complex. However, we now do a comparison between tenders which involves looking at both these percentages and the spread of prices in the *activity schedule* to identify any anomalies or excessive loading.

The lessons we learnt from these early contracts were that

- they will not save you man hours during the currency of the contract, although overall, from award to settlement of final account, they are probably neutral. The advantage is that issues are agreed as the contract progresses and all parties can typically walk away from a job within a month or two of Completion, rather than the year or two it would typically take under traditional forms.
- lack of familiarity from Contractors meant that the full benefits of using the NEC/ECC were not being realised. This is still a problem with some of them. There was also a cultural issue in that part of the reason for using the NEC was that we wanted to work with and alongside our Contractors, not against them. This took a couple of years to really put across and for trust to develop.

- as a client, when a variation occurred, we would traditionally tend to decide how much we would pay based on its value to us. The NEC/ECC and its method of evaluating compensation events is not consistent with this approach and highlights to both parties more clearly the true costs involved. In the long term, this is not a bad thing as it educates our own technical staff just how much a change can cost. It therefore puts an onus on us to decide exactly what we want and to specify it precisely before a contract is put out to tender.

These are short term disadvantages for long term benefits and they are being realised.

We have not found any ongoing disadvantages from using the NEC and ECC, although we do feel that we are possibly not achieving the full benefits because

- of the continued lack of familiarity by some *Contractors*
- some *Contractors* will not use it back-to-back with their Subcontractors. This, in our view, can inhibit the overall management of the contract and puts the *Contractor* at risk.
- the standard of programmes submitted to us for acceptance is generally disappointing compared with standards expected by the ECC. This is partly a function of the software used — it would be unreasonable to insist that *Contractors* use a particular type of software when the ECC is not the predominant contract under which they do business.

Additionally, while the time scales impose a good discipline on the parties and prevent issues dragging on, at times they are hard to achieve. However, there is the facility within the ECC to extend them.

The advantages we found and continue to find are that

- it has fulfilled our original reasons for using it i.e. it can be used across a range of technical disciplines with any extent of *Contractor* design and that it is neutral, so we and *Contractors* can obtain independent advice and training on it.

- it means what it says and you can take what the contract says at face value. The lack of case law helps in this respect. As a result, we have modified it very little and will continue to use it in its near pure form for the foreseeable future.
- it certainly helps relationships at site level because it provides personnel with a framework for project managing the contract. Providing people are competent and have an understanding of project management, they do not need to be an expert or have great experience to properly manage an NEC contract as it leads them through the necessary processes.
- it gives us much greater knowledge of the most likely out turn Price and date for Completion at any point during the construction process than do conventional contracts. It also enables us to make choices about what the best way to proceed is when circumstances cause things to deviate from what was originally planned. This is because the compensation event procedure allows us to ask for quotations based on different assumptions.
- while we traditionally have less disputes than the civil engineering industry, we probably have even less now. For instance, we have not had any ongoing disputes or had to refer a single dispute to adjudication.

As a result we have progressively increased the size of contract we have felt comfortable using the ECC on, with the largest individual contract being awarded on it worth just under £50 million. When we introduced the NEC, we would let our contracts on the price-based options (Options A and B). Over the last couple of years we have moved away from these options towards the target contract with activity schedule, as we feel this further reinforces the philosophy of working alongside our *Contractors* for mutual benefit.

THE PROJECT MANAGER'S VIEW

Simon McGrail is the company cost manager for the Project and Construction Management Practice, GDG Management Ltd. GDG are currently concluding a coldstore and warehouse facility in excess of £25 million for Müller Dairies where the Engineering and Construction Contract, Option A, priced contract with activity schedule was employed exclusively in a Construction Management environment.

In 1996 GDG Management were appointed by Müller Dairies to project manage a new coldstore and distribution warehouse at their Market Drayton production facility, a complex project incorporating automated materials handling equipment and coldstore construction to a high volume distribution warehouse. GDG recommended the adoption of the New Engineering Contract for both consultant appointments and construction contracts. Since the formation of GDG in 1990, the practice had been reviewing available standard forms of contract for one that would complement the company's ethos of transparency, fairness and good practical management. Therefore, following the Latham Report's endorsement of the NEC as a 'fair' contract the practice took note and undertook to examine this new contract in detail. It was subsequently agreed that the Müller project would be procured as a Construction Management contract, however there was no independently drafted contract form available in the UK. Following their review of the NEC, GDG felt that the ECC could be employed even though it had not been drafted specifically for Construction Management.

Since that time GDG have become participants of NEC user groups and working parties, advocating the use of the contract to its clients, while acknowledging that as a young form it requires some refinement and, most importantly, a philosophical change of attitude of participants from traditional contractual positions.

The Engineering and Construction Contract was accepted by Müller and has been successfully employed on the multimillion pound Construction Management project. This success was not without difficulties in administering the contract and required the

66

Employer to embrace the contract as much as the consultants and eventually the trade contractors.

Müller's commitment to this new form was demonstrated early on in the development when, upon GDG advice, Müller sponsored a series of *Contractor* workshops for potential trade contractors to explain the contract form, the fact that it is an active participant in the management of a project and the mechanics and procedures set out therein. The workshops covered subjects such as the contractual basis of the *Contractor's* programme; the *activity schedule*, its importance and how it facilitated payments; the preparation of compensation event quotations and the meaning of Actual Cost. The workshops proved invaluable. However, these alone were insufficient for all parties to truly understand the changes, in principle, of how a 'compensation event' or variation should be calculated.

The importance of a 100% complete statement of what is required prior to procurement is a requirement of the NEC that is most often underestimated. The fact that an omission or change to Works Information requires immediate attention means that it cannot be rolled up into global settlements and therefore makes all parties accountable for their actions. This requirement dovetails ideally with the procurement philosophies of Construction Management. The fact that Construction Management procures the works trade by trade enables the complete design intent of the NEC to be adopted without delay to the start of a project or risk where 100% design of a total project is not possible due to its scale or complexity.

Once on site the most common misunderstandings GDG encountered were as follows.

The *activity schedule*

This would often be prepared merely as a tendering requirement. Insufficient thought was given to how the activities would actually be broken down on site into completed tasks and thereby provide cashflow in line with progress or, how individual tasks may need to be grouped into an activity, because if one task was not completed it was impossible to complete others. It was also often thought that once an *activity schedule* was agreed it was 'cast in stone', whereas, even though a compensation event may have a zero forecast cost, it could still result in a revised sequence of works and therefore a revised programme and consequently a revised *activity schedule*.

Contract Data Part II

The Contract Data Part II completed during tendering by *Contractors* would often have to be revised following post-tender meetings. The most common misunderstanding was that this was in some way a new form of daywork rather than a basis for forecasting costs for a compensation event. There was often confusion over which percentages reimbursed *Contractors* for on-site preliminaries; why there was not an opportunity to include tradesman rates for work on site and the fact that Subcontractors' mark up would not be accepted in a rate for people but must be incorporated into the *fee percentage*.

Quotations for compensation events

The mechanics of forecasting Actual Costs for a compensation event would be confused with a lump sum quote where the method of calculating the *Contractor's* quotation is 'none of the *Project Manager's* business'. Furthermore, the principle that Actual Cost was as defined by the contract, not 'that's what my Subcontractor has quoted me', also necessitated reminders of the examples illustrated in the *Contractor's* workshops.

What was quite clear from these misunderstandings was that the financial management of compensation events was the most difficult to explain and be absorbed until put into practice. These difficulties, however, were purely ones of mechanics. The environment that the contract provided allowed the process to be successful even when first time users were having difficulties understanding the specifics.

The disadvantages from GDG's view were limited, however the fact that a specific Construction Management form is not available made recognition of a master programme and cross charging trade *Contractors* unsatisfactory. An NEC working party is currently addressing these issues. GDG also identified that the application of the Working Area Overhead percentage as the vehicle for reimbursing the *Contractor* for on-site preliminaries can be iniquitous to both the *Employer* and the *Contractor*. Finally, the absence of a short or minor form for small value and simple works left a gap in the suite of contracts which remains unaddressed.

A major benefit of the NEC form for GDG however, is the *activity schedule* option where works are focussed on clearly defined deliverables: a principle adopted by GDG for both *Consultant* and *Contractor* appointments. This option removes the contentious issue of whether a proportion of an item of work is due for payment or not as the activity is either complete or it is not. This mechanism also focusses contractors and consultants, alike, to complete a task by the programmed date in order to receive payment.

The compensation event procedures also provide clear accountability for causes of change. Omission and errors can no longer be hidden away.

The fact that the contract is written in plain English allows all parties to understand what is required of them without constant concern of the legal interpretation. The early warning of potential compensation events allows implications of cost and programme to be considered while there is still an opportunity to make an informed decision. Furthermore, the early warning procedure is a procedure within the contract itself, not a project procedure grafted on somewhere else in the contract documents.

Payment terms are prompt and contractor cashflow requirements are reflected by the *Contractor* having drafting control over the activity schedule, while the *Employer* is protected by the clearly defined deliverables in the *activity schedule*.

The response times for communications and compensations events resulted in a higher administrative burden for all parties than was expected at the outset. However, it resulted in contentious issues being addressed and resolved at the point that they occurred rather than remaining unresolved and resulting in post-contract claims and disputes.

Participants who embraced the philosophy of 'mutual trust and co-operation' found that, while the new terminology and calculation of compensation events was a steep learning curve, the atmosphere of team management and problem solving far outweighed these difficulties and resulted in a demanding project being completed without any referrals to Adjudication, Arbitration or Litigation. Final Accounts were agreed promptly upon completion of a trade contractor's works and many trade contractors have become repeat providers to both Müller and GDG.

GDG, Müller and the trade contractors have all learned a considerable amount about the contract and how to administer it from using it, which no workshop could replicate. When GDG recommended its use to Müller, they thought they were recommending a fairer, less confrontational way of doing business. This was proven to be the case.

All parties learned, however, that for the contract to work it must be embraced in its entirety and that its spirit is often more important than its specific. If old attitudes and positions are adopted, the principle for employing the NEC is lost. However, because the procedures were clearly set out and the rights and remedies were immediate, the project continued to be managed effectively in spite of the few resisters that were encountered.

GDG cannot foresee any long term disadvantages to the NEC and believe that its wider use would contribute to a more united, open, communicative industry and provide the environment for better predictability, stability and efficiency.

The Consultant's View

WS Atkins Transportation Engineering administer Area 2 of the United Kingdom Road Network on behalf of UK Highways Agency. Having let two small value contracts under Option B, the priced contract with bill of quantities, they then let a £2.5 million resurfacing scheme under Option A, the priced contract with activity schedule. Andrew Williams is the deputy divisional manager and was delegated the Project Manager's powers, David Beer was the Supervisor with David Coles the Deputy Supervisor.

The reason for our use of the ECC is the desire for UK Highways Agency to progressively introduce its use across the network as one of a number of contract options available. However, as Consultants we supported this initiative as we saw two advantages: firstly, it will enable us to do a better job of managing and controlling contracts on our client's behalf, and secondly, it will lead to an overall reduction in construction costs. This has been confirmed by our experiences. We would like to think, as Consultants, that we work with Contractors and are fair to them regardless of the conditions of contract under which our schemes are let. In this respect the ECC, with its philosophy of co-operation, more closely reflects the way we in which we like to work.

The Option A contract was for £2.5 million resurfacing job with ancillary works — waterproofing bridge decks, renewing the safety fencing, the street lighting and cabling and hardening the central reservation — on the M5 motorway at the intersection between it, the M4 motorway and the A38, one of the principal roads serving the city of Bristol.

During the tender period, the tendering Contractors stated that they could not take off some quantities with sufficient accuracy, so we issued more detailed drawings. We also limited their risk in two areas, these being repairs to bridge decks prior to waterproofing, and replacement of electrical equipment in lighting columns. In each case, the extent of the works could not be determined until the works were under way, so a maximum amount of work was specified beyond which a compensation event would occur.

71

Because of the location of the *works*, minimising disruption to the traffic was a high priority and therefore assessment of Contractors was weighted 40% towards the quality of the tender which included their submitted programme and traffic management proposals. The tenders also included a lane rental element to minimise the duration of the *works*. Both the quality of their tender and the total of their tender Prices meant that Associated Asphalt were awarded the contract.

We specified that only the Shorter Schedule of Cost Components would be used. On receiving back the tenders, we did an analysis of the effect of various tendered percentages which are applied to the shorter Schedule when a compensation event occurs. We believe the tendered percentages were high, possibly because we had not stated this as an area which we would evaluate. In future, we will state how these will be taken into account in the tender assessment.

Having awarded the contract, we held a partnering workshop that was beneficial in building relationships that would aid the smooth running of the contract. After this, our key people were invited by the *Contractor* to attend a day's training on the ECC at their premises. We also held our own training seminars. Partly as a result of these, both parties adapted our existing pro-formas to match the requirements of the ECC and we spent time with the *Contractor* ensuring that his programme was acceptable. It also gave us useful advice on how to quickly and amicably agree compensation events.

Price certainty is very important to the Highways Agency. One of the amendments to the Contract by the Highways Agency was the removal of the weather compensation event, which meant that the *Contractor* took all the risk of bad weather: this caused some irritation to the *Contractor* early in the contract when bad weather was encountered. Fortunately, the weather for the remainder of the contract was good, but in future we would recommend this clause be reinstated as, in our opinion, it places uncontrollable and therefore unpriceable risk on the *Contractor* for short duration high intensity work of this type. It could also force the *Contractor* into doing work in unsuitable conditions to the detriment of quality, which in turn would effect relationships. In extreme circumstances it could lead to frustration of the contract. That said, we are aware that the Highways Agency believes that the *Contractor* was, in this instance, best placed to minimise the effect of the bad weather and that they were very pleased with the way in which the effects of poor weather were minimised by the *Contractor*.

When a technical problem occurred, we would have an early warning meeting to resolve the issue as rapidly as possible. Generally these meeting were on an informal basis and would have occurred on any lane rental scheme whatever the form of contract: the ECC just puts them on a contractual footing. We did, however, have weekly meetings to wrap up issues. Because every communication has to be 'in a form which can read, copied and recorded', we adopted the principle of agreeing orally and confirming and summarising in writing. This led to reduced administration. The action applied to early warnings and compensation events, which, because of the nature of the work, were usually contractually notified on the same form. The majority of compensation events were assessed on records as to do otherwise would have delayed the progress of the *works*.

Use of activity schedules saved us the use of a quantity surveyor throughout the duration of the contract and we would imagine the situation was similar for the *Contractor*. Rather than a week plus to agree the monthly evaluation it was almost a five minute walk round site. This reduced our site supervision costs, and resulted in savings for the client.

The contract finished on the date originally planned and the final account was settled within two and a half working weeks of this date, although it has to be said that no major technical problems were encountered and there was no consequent delay and disruption. We found that the language and procedures do help to break down the barriers between those supervising the work and those actually doing it. Overall, the ECC reinforced the way in which we liked to work.

In terms of future use, we will shortly be trialling the use of Option C, the target contract with activity schedule, although its application on contracts where the works are well defined and subject to small risk is limited. Further, the costs of setting up and administrating open book accounting may be excessive on small value contracts. We see the majority of our future contracts being let on Option A, the priced contract with activity schedule, of the ECC.

We have also had developed for us a term maintenance contract, based on Option A of the ECC. It includes performance-based activities — for example, the *Contractor* is responsible for keeping grass length below 150 mm, whereas previously we would tell him when to cut an area of grass — and time-based activities: for example, the *Contractor* has to clean out gullies at a certain time of the year and we audit the quality of his work, as well as a *priced schedule of rates* from which we can call off individual operations. Additionally, we have strengthened the programming requirements to facilitate greater control over the *works*. Again this should reduce our operating costs, yet enhance our ability to manage the network on our client's behalf.

We have since had post contract discussions with both winning and losing contractors for three ECC contracts. From these discussions, the following contract strategies are due to be trialled in the near future, namely

- requesting a base price for Option A and C works with minimum risk transfer to the *Contractor*, and 'extra over' prices for identified risk items such as weather, so that the client can decide whether to pay for the risk
- encouraging innovation by the *Contractor* by allowing a long mobilisation period of approximately three months together with an incentive on Option A and B contracts whereby the *Contractor* has a share of all savings
- providing an incentive to the Consultant and *Contractor* to reduce costs on site by a cost sharing arrangements for cost reduction identified during the construction phase.

THE QUANTITY SURVEYOR'S VIEW

Mike Attridge is a chartered quantity surveyor with over 20 years' experience in the construction industry. Having worked as a site-based surveyor for a national civil engineering contractor, Mike joined C. M. Needleman & Partners, a London-based firm of chartered quantity surveyors, in 1986. This led to his involvement with the cost planning, procurement and construction phases of the Heathrow Express Rail Link, the new high-speed rail service between London's Paddington station and Heathrow airport. In 1993 Mike was given responsibility for the preparation of tender documentation and tender invitations for the tunnelling works within Heathrow Airport. The contract was awarded in March 1994 and, at the time, was the largest contract let under the NEC in Britain. Mike led the contract administration team reporting directly to BAA's Project Manager until November 1996 when he joined Union Railways Limited: London and Continental Railway's subsidiary responsible for overseeing the design, procurement and construction of the new high-speed Channel Tunnel Rail Link between London St. Pancras and Folkestone. This project has recently let approximately £800 million of civil engineering work on the NEC's Engineering and Construction Contract. He now works as an independent consultant to the construction industry.

Contract C/D as it was known was the principal civil engineering package for BAA's new Heathrow Express Rail Link. It required the construction of approximately 10 km of new running tunnel and two new below-ground stations, one serving Heathrow Airport's Terminals 1, 2 and 3 and the other Terminal 4. The running tunnels were to be constructed using traditional techniques, while the stations were to be constructed using techniques associated with the New Austrian Tunnelling Method.

The contract was tendered competitively and let in March 1994 for approximately £60 million making it at the time the largest contract let in the UK on the NEC form of contract. The design of the 'permanent works' at contract award was substantially complete, the *Employer* having taken responsibility for design under the contract. It was therefore anticipated that the incidence of change would be low, which logically led to the decision to use the NEC's Main Option A, the priced contract with activity schedule. This option is effectively a 'lump sum' contractual arrangement under which the *Contractor* carries the financial risk of being able to complete the works for the tendered Prices, subject only to any adjustments resulting from compensation events.

There was only a very short mobilisation period on Contract C/D and the formal administrative systems and procedures for dealing with compensation events in a consistent manner both across the entire contract (which was geographically widespread) and in accordance with the NEC had not been fully established. Unfortunately, compensation events began to occur and *Contractor's* notifications of compensation events started to arrive in greater numbers and at a greater frequency than had been anticipated. One of our first tasks — and one which, with the benefit of hindsight, should have been carried out before contract award — was the drafting up of administrative procedures and the establishment of systems to reflect the procedural requirements and time demands of the contract. No other form of contract regulates the participants' actions and decisions so tightly by not only specifying the time constraints but also by the setting down the basis for their actions and decisions. Consequently, internal procedures were prepared covering such subjects as early warnings, communications, acceptance of Defects and, most importantly, the administration of compensation events. An important part of this exercise was the setting up of a computer-based system for tracking compensation events through the various contractual stages from notification through to implementation and the recording of the agreed financial and time effects of these events.

Although there were no formal partnering arrangements on Contract C/D, relationships at site between the *Project Manager's* and the *Contractor's* teams were good. This stemmed more from the qualities of the senior managers on both sides and the mutual respect that existed rather than directly from any collaborative working engendered by the contract. Having said this, the early warning procedure proved a major factor in cementing site relationships closer to the work-face. Before the contract began, while recognising the obvious benefits to both Parties of the early warning system, I had been somewhat cynical of its chances of success in a 'live' context, particularly on a lump sum contract. Its success was probably due to the realisation by the *Contractor* that the early warning procedure was far superior to his existing 'Request For Further Information' and 'Technical Query and Answer' procedures. It actually gives him the power to instruct the *Project Manager* to attend an early warning meeting at which the matter causing concern is tabled, options for limiting its impact on the *works* are considered and avoiding or mitigating actions agreed. The *Project Manager* then prepares a record of the decisions made and the actions agreed at these meetings. Initially there were a couple of instances where early warning meetings were called after the time had passed for being able to influence the impact of the matter and, at the other extreme, people calling early warning meetings to resolve simple technical issues. However, once bedded in, the early warning system went a long way in promoting collaborative working and prevented any 'ducking' of the issues and 'benefit of hindsight' arguments commonly run under more traditional contracts.

Two areas where, with hindsight, the collaborative working principle embodied in the NEC should have been extended to greater benefit was with the preparation by the *Contractor* of quotations for compensation events and revised programmes. In the case of the former, the *Project Manager* would instruct the *Contractor* to prepare quotations. There would then be little contact made over the stipulated two week period (under the first edition of the NEC) while the *Contractor* was preparing his detailed assessment of the financial and time effects of the related compensation event. It was hardly surprising therefore that when quotations were submitted there was nearly always something that the *Project Manager's* team did not understand or felt the need to question. Most frequently, these related to the *Contractor's* assumptions behind his forecasts of the effects of the compensation event on resource or productivity levels. A similar problem was encountered with the preparation of revised programmes by the *Contractor*. The result was that a lot of time would be spent trying to nail down quotations for compensation events and revisions to the Accepted Programmes. This led to frustration on both sides of the contractual divide. The solution must be for the planners and quantity surveyors from both sides to work together in a much more integrated manner forming essentially a single department responsible for the production of revised programmes and quotations for compensation events. This may have seemed quite radical only a short time ago but today would appear entirely consistent with the growth of partnering (and its removal of duplicated effort) and the greater prevalence of target cost contracts where the financial risk is shared between Employer and Contractor.

Difficulties were experienced with the detailed assessment of the financial and time effects of compensation events and criticism can be levelled at both sides. The first thing to note here is that this is not a problem peculiar to the NEC. Traditionally a great deal of effort is spent arguing over such matters as the applicability of tendered rates and who owns any float in the programme when it becomes necessary to assess any financial or time entitlement due to the Contractor. While the NEC has swept away these particular problems, it does require the *Contractor* to make assessments of the financial and time effects of compensation events at the time they arise. Invariably this means such assessments are based on the *Contractor's* forecast of the effects of the compensation event on his costs and programme, rather than on records. What's more, once the *Project Manager* has accepted the *Contractor's* quotation, there is no retrospective re-visit of the forecast should later recorded information show it to have been wrong. The NEC justifies this potential imbalance by pointing to the advantages of such an approach including

- improved cash flow for the *Contractor*
- greater certainty of outcome for both Parties
- the increased incentive for the *Contractor* to control the cost and time effects of a compensation event within the pre-agreed parameters set down in the accepted quotation
- the elimination of the effort needed to maintain extensive records for use as the basis for a retrospective assessment (claim) of the financial and time effects of a variation.

If the *Contractor* is organised and, in particular, maintains a regularly updated programme to the standards required by the NEC, then it is unlikely that the *Contractor* will get a forecast horribly wrong. Nevertheless on Contract C/D the fear of under-assessing the effects of a compensation event was very real for the *Contractor*. His initial defence was to provide quotations that only dealt with the direct effects of the compensation event i.e. those effects that could be relatively easily assessed. It was commonplace to receive quotations marked as excluding the effects of prolongation, disruption and risk. This was clearly unsatisfactory and undermined a principal benefit of the NEC, namely greater certainty for both *Contractor* and *Employer* at any stage of the contract of the time and financial outcome of the project. Consequently, quotations containing such an exclusion were rejected. This is fine to a point, but the contract requires the *Project Manager* to rectify this now uncertain situation by making his own assessment of the effects of the compensation event. This is not a discretionary right – indeed it cannot be if the principal benefit of the NEC mentioned above is to be realised. It does however place additional responsibility and demands on the *Project Manager's* team. There is really no answer to this other than to hope that after one or two less than favourable *Project Manager's* assessments the *Contractor* realises that it is in his own commercial interest to comply with the compensation event provisions.

Having persuaded the *Contractor* to include not only the direct financial and time effects of compensation events in his quotations, but also the indirect effects, the next challenge for the *Contractor* was to convince the *Project Manager's* team that apparently trivial compensation events could have the major financial implications they claimed. Maintaining a good Accepted Programme helped the *Contractor* in this respect, as he could then more easily demonstrate which activities were on or close to the critical path. The *Project Manager* then could (and should under any form of contract) be constantly 'scouting' ahead on the lookout for events that have the potential to adversely impact these activities.

The periods stated in the contract for the preparation and submission of quotations for compensation events proved difficult for the *Contractor* to comply with and this was a very organised *Contractor*. There were a number of reasons for this. First of all, compensation events tend to be a bit like London buses: one week there will be none and the next week ten all arrive on the same day. This presents a problem for the *Contractor* in terms of having the necessary resources on site to deal with the fluctuations in workload. Given this problem, I am at a total loss to understand why in the second edition of the NEC the drafters have sought to expressly exclude the *Contractor's* costs of preparing quotations for compensation events. However, two other factors made compliance within the stipulated time-scales difficult under the first edition of the NEC, namely

- the *Contractor* was only allowed two weeks to submit a quotation, whereas in the second edition it is now three
- there was no provision for extending the time periods, which there is now, if the *Project Manager* and the *Contractor* agree.

It is also worth noting that there is a skills issue here: quantity surveyors that are familiar with resource-based estimating techniques (as required by the NEC) as opposed to assessing everything on unit rates and records (as is normal under more traditional contract forms) are a scarce commodity.

In the recently published Construction Task Force Report *Rethinking construction* it stated that 'the industry must help clients to understand the need for resources to be concentrated up-front on projects if greater efficiency and quality are to be delivered'. I agree. In our project, many minor deficiencies in the Works Information were not discovered before they adversely impacted on the *works*. Because they were discovered at the time of doing the work, the knock-on effects on subsequent work caused delay, disruption and therefore additional cost which often exceeded the direct costs of putting it right. The NEC illustrated the effects of poor quality documentation and, with hindsight, more time should have been spent up-front seeking to eradicate these deficiencies. For all the justifiable criticisms levelled at bill of quantities, those in-the-know appreciate that there is no better means of checking the completeness of the drawings and specification than the discipline associated with the preparation of a bill of quantities. The elimination of this process can represent a major risk on those main options of the NEC that do not require the preparation of a bill of quantities by the *Employer's* team.

I would sum up my NEC experiences to date as follows. The principal benefit of this form of contract is the greater certainty of outcome it should provide at any stage of the construction process for both *Employer and Contractor*. This greater certainty is derived from the greater control over cost and time that flows from the heavy emphasis placed on strong project management. It must however be realised that this greater control is only achieved by collaborative working and strict compliance with the provisions of the contract. This can be very demanding on the Parties if they have not appreciated in advance the fundamental differences between the NEC and more traditional contracts, particularly if the job is plagued by compensation events. I personally believe the additional effort required by both Parties in pursuit of the potential benefits offered by the NEC is worth expending but that they need to embark down this path with their eyes and minds firmly open.

THE CONTRACTOR'S VIEW

Paul Bates is senior project manager for Wates Construction in their South West Region. He is responsible for the construction of a new synthetic chemistry building for Bristol University due for completion in August 1999.

The building consists of 16 laboratory modules on four floors, with a basement level of plant and another level of plant on the roof. Each laboratory has six identical fume cupboards and there are three specialist cupboards on the lower level. These fume cupboards need a lot of air and four large fume ducts run from the bottom to the top of the building to satisfy this need. Mechanical and electrical services are a fundamental part of the building. The client wanted a high degree of price certainty on the project and the building has to be ready for the start of the academic year in October 1999.

In August 1997, we, together with the fume cupboard suppliers and the potential mechanical and electrical works contractors, were appointed to work with the designers and end users as part of a co-located team taking part in value engineering, risk analysis and buildability exercises. No detailed design had taken place at this point. The financial basis for our selection was on a tendered fixed fee for this pre-construction phase, the estimated cost of preliminaries for the construction phase and our tendered *fee percentage* which would be applied to compensation events. However, this only accounted for a third of the selection criteria. The other factors taken into account were the attitude, skills and experience which we could bring to the project.

In November 1997 work began on site and we, as part of the pre-construction fixed fee contract, managed the demolition of the existing car park and some other enabling work on the client's behalf. Because of some delays in detailing, the enabling works were extended to include the substructure of the new building.

By Spring 1998, 92% of the cost of the building had been securely designed and tendered. While we put out and received back the tendered subcontract packages, there was full disclosure to the client of these costs. We also disclosed our on-site costs for managing the works, preliminaries etc. The construction contract was let in May 1998 under Option B, the priced contract with bill of quantities, of the NEC Engineering and Construction Contract (ECC) at an initial value of £11.5 million. If the client had been unhappy with our performance up to that point then we would not have been awarded the construction contract. The fume cupboard suppliers and mechanical and electrical contractors, who had been involved with us in the pre-construction stages, became our Subcontractors, as the client wanted single point responsibility. The use and contribution of the ECC to the eventual success of the project has, therefore, to be put in context: it is part of the answer, not the whole answer.

Prior to starting on site, we had two half-day seminars by people who had already worked under the ECC. These were delivered to the whole team, not just us, the *Contractor*. One thing that was stressed to us was the administrative requirements of the contract. As a team, we therefore developed a system of standard forms. We also assigned two quantity surveyors to administer the early warning and compensation event procedures. Initially, we tried to communicate as we thought the contract required: 'in a form that can be read, copied and recorded' i.e. writing. We found this to be too much of a burden, so started to discuss things before writing them down. While this saves bureaucracy, the administrative requirements are still daunting. We tend to confirm verbal instructions on technical queries sheets, which are then rolled up once a week in an early warning notification from the *Project Manager*.

We and specialist Subcontractors use early warning as a matter of course. The smaller domestic Subcontractors are unfamiliar with the ECC, so we tend to early warn to the *Project Manager* on their behalf. The early warning meetings, which need not be big formal affairs, force us to discuss problems with others and think through the consequences, rather than just getting on with the work.

Because we have two quantity surveyors on site dedicated to the task, with exception of one or two of the more complex compensation events, we have been able to agree the time and cost effects within the time scales stipulated in the contract. Our quantity surveyors have tended to discuss and agree costs with the *Project Manager's* quantity surveyors before formally submitting the quotation to the *Project Manager* for his acceptance. On a building site, you tend to get frequent small value changes. Assessing these through the Schedule of Cost Components would be time consuming and many of the relatively unsophisticated subcontractors would be unable to do it. Having a bill of quantities helps in this respect as we can use tendered rates.

Our formal Accepted Programme is four pages of A3 which is updated when requested by the *Project Manager* or whenever it no longer corresponds to what is happening on site. We issue it first for discussion and take account of any comments both from the Subcontractors' and the client's side before issuing it formally. It has not been updated for every compensation event with a time implication for obvious reasons. Our short term programmes are derived from the Accepted Programme and these are distributed to every member of the project team.

Summarising, the main disadvantage with the ECC is the amount of bureaucracy and the on-site administration needed during the construction phase. The beauty of the ECC is that there are no surprises for anybody and you strike agreements as you go along, so the client knows what it is costing him as the project progresses; we and our Subcontractors know what we are getting paid and whether we are making a profit. It also gives us more positive cash flow and the final account should be agreed within a month of Completion. The amount of time spent post Completion should therefore be reduced and, overall, from the award of the contract to the settlement of final account, the total administrative man-hours could end up less than under a JCT form.

Our view of the ECC is that it reinforces the way we like to work: co-operatively with our clients and subcontractors, but on its own it will not create co-operation. It may not work with a confrontational contractor and it is not a panacea for the industry's problems. It does, however, make people aware of the consequences of an action or event very quickly and imposes a discipline on the participants to resolve it quickly. The good contractors should not struggle with it and we are comfortable with it.

THE SUBCONTRACTOR'S VIEW

IEI Ltd were employed as a subcontractor for the completion of the design, supply, installation and commissioning of the complete Building Services for the terminal building at Southampton Eastleigh Airport. The Employer was BAA plc who let the contract on Option A, the priced contract with activity schedules, of the first edition of the New Engineering Contract. The main Contractor let the subcontract for building services under the same option of the subcontract form. Steve Dwyer was their site-based quantity surveyor.

This was the first tender under the NEC that IEI had been asked to complete. At the time, the company estimators and surveyors had no experience or knowledge of the form, its requirements or pitfalls. It was therefore necessary to obtain a complete copy and quickly assimilate the contents.

Our initial reading produced a very pessimistic report as, in common with the majority of the industry at that time, we could not believe that the construction team could work together as closely as was obviously required by the contract. We also felt that the time scales for pricing compensation events — one week for the Subcontractor under the first edition — were tight and could be difficult to comply with if there was a high level of change during the contract.

We were pleased however that there was a clear distinction in the contract between the construction team — the *Contractor* and his Subcontractors — and the *Project Manager*. We believed that this could promote a better working relationship as all team members would become aware of their reliance on others to firstly complete the *works* in time and secondly to obtain any benefits from using the NEC. We also believed that the method of calculating stage payments — the *activity schedule* — was eminently fair and should produce a positive cash flow provided we maintained our planned progress.

Once on site, I think both parties were unwilling to believe that the required level of co-operation could work. We were wary of each other and, to an extent, maintained the confrontational approach common on other forms of contract. Without co-operation, we found it was not possible to effectively programme the *works* and maintain the tendered programme. Therefore both the main *Contractor's* and our cash flows were adversely effected. Also, our tendered staged payment document (the *activity schedule*) was not detailed enough to allow a realistic cash flow. This taught us a valuable lesson: future contracts would be more comprehensively analysed so that a more detailed *activity schedule* could be prepared in order that our cash flow remained positive through out the contract.

The process of agreeing quotations for compensation events helped to persuade the main *Contractor* of the benefits of co-operation. He began to realise that without our programming input, the works were unlikely to be completed by the Completion Date and that he was unlikely to obtain adequate extensions to the Completion Date due to the compensation events that arose.

Our worries about the time scales for submitting quotations on compensation events proved to be unfounded. At all times, we were able to respond within the period for submission with a firm cost or agree to an extension due to the complexity and size of the additional work. However, this was at the cost of myself, a senior member of the surveying staff, spending a disproportionate amount of time on this contract compared with a contract let under a traditional form of contract.

A benefit of the hard work during the contract, which we did not appreciate at the time, was that the final account was agreed and settled within one month of Completion. This was because of the emphasis of the NEC on pre-assessing and agreeing the cost and time effects of changes prior to doing the work.

As the contract progressed and the benefits of co-operation became obvious, working relationships improved. For instance, when a catering area was added to the contract, the main *Contractor* spent some time discussing and agreeing the programme required to meet the tight deadline for the opening of the terminal.

This co-operation has led to the two companies working together on many other contracts as equal partners and, we believe, it has led to a change in the *Contractor's* general attitude towards subcontractors. They appear to no longer view us as a necessary evil.

This contract was time driven and demanding on all involved. It could easily have become confrontational and resulted in a large claim. It did not and this was largely due to the use of the New Engineering Contract. Provided attention is focussed at tender on the *activity schedule* and during the contract on the submission and agreement of quotation for compensation events, then the advantages far outweigh the disadvantages. We would willingly enter into further subcontracts using this form of contract.

Part III

Implementation

Effective and efficient implementation of any project starts with the identification of a need; justifying the need with a proper business case; defining the function/purpose that the project has to fulfil and examining options to fulfil that need. It is only after the construction option has been justified, that the most suitable contract strategy can be selected and developed (section 1.3) and it is only then that the provisions within the ECC can aid the effective and efficient implementation of a project. If the contract strategy is severely flawed, it is unlikely that the procedures for stimulating good management in the ECC will save the project from failing to meet its objectives.

A number of interviewees have expressed the view that in untrained hands the ECC could be dangerous as it requires intelligence in its use, because it is just as much a project management tool as a conditions of contract and a tool is only as good as the person using it. Regrettably, the research sample identified some examples to justify this view.

While some of the authors of the ECC would claim that it is applicable across the whole construction industry, this author feels that there are three situations where use of the ECC is inappropriate.

- When it is thought that the *Employer* or their contractors are unable to make the cultural changes towards a more collaborative style of contracting. The research indicated that the ECC reinforces co-operation, but cannot create the will to co-operate. Using the ECC without that will goes against the ethos of the contract. This has implications on the selection of the *Contractor* and personnel from all sides of the industry (section 3.1.3).
- The ECC gives both parties the tools to project manage effectively, but if either side cannot project manage properly, then use of the ECC will leave them exposed, as they will not be able to conform to the contract's requirements. Unfortunately, it is human nature for people to regard themselves as good managers, regardless of their capabilities.
- The ECC currently lacks clauses for the control of multiple interfaces between different contract packages e.g. the construction management approach (section 1.3.1.4). At the time of writing this book, the NEC Panel are writing clauses to overcome this deficiency. If the reader intends to use the ECC for this purpose and wishes to write their own clauses to cover this eventuality, then the general guidelines for writing additional clauses in Option Z (section 1.3.2) should be followed.

Part III of this book leads the reader and potential user through the changes necessary to gain the most from using the ECC. The majority of these changes should be in place within the first month of the contract. This includes understanding the ECC's principal clauses, how they fit together and stimulates good management as outlined in Part I of this guide. This Part is divided into five sections: pre-tender; preparing the tender; evaluating the tender; post award and the construction phase. However, this user's guide should be taken as a whole and it is recommended that users do not use one section in isolation as issues mentioned in the later sections may have been developed from the earlier sections. Then when addressing a specific aspect of implementation, the section which addresses that aspect can be referred to. For this reason, and to prevent duplication, there is cross referencing between sections.

Examples of best and not so good practice from real projects examined in the research are given in boxes. Much of this information was given in confidence, and therefore the source matter is not attributed.

3.1 PRE-TENDER

The main actions necessary for the *Employer* to undertake prior to putting a contract out to tender are

- selection of an appropriate contract strategy. This was considered in section 1.3.
- preparation of the contract documentation, which includes
  - o completion of Part I of the Contract Data
  - o consideration of other issues.

3.1.1 Preparation of the contract documentation

One of the key factors leading to successful project implementation, under any conditions of contract, is good contract documentation. As one research report from Australia[*] stated: 'The greatest cause of claims and disputes in the construction industry is related to problems in contract documentation, including errors, contradiction, ambiguity and the late supply of documents, which give rise to delays and inefficiencies and hence claims'. Another research project in Canada[†] indicated that, on average, Employers pay three times as much for the equivalent work introduced after the contract is let compared with work included in the original contract

---

[*] Australian Construction Services (1988). Department of Administrative Services and several other particpants, *Strategies for the reduction of claims and disputes in the construction industry. A research report*, Queensland.

[†] Revay S. G. (1992). Can construction claims be avoided? In Fenn P. and Gameson R. (eds), *Construction conflict and resolution*. E & FN Spon.

documentation. The reasons for this include the additional on-site costs due to delays and loss of productivity i.e. disruption.

A number of interviewees from the research sample expressed the view that the ECC makes deficiencies in documentation more apparent and the effect more immediate and evident. This is because

- clause 60.1 (1) makes it clear that any change to the Works Information is the *Employer's* liability
- clause 63.7, which states the legal principle called the *contra preferentum* rule. That is, a change to the Works Information is interpreted in the light least favourable to the party who prepared it.
- the time and cost effects are calculated and agreed closer to the time of the change than is normal under traditional conditions of contract
- the cost effects of an individual compensation event include not only the direct costs, but also the indirect costs resulting from prolongation and disruption.

In the words of one interviewee, 'there are no hiding places within the NEC', so poor documentation can be traced back to its originator. Designers beware!

It should be stressed that the way in which the Works Information is written should flow from the contract strategy. For instance, it would be foolish to design the *works* and then, once completed, decide to allocate design responsibility to the *Contractor*.

The following steps are recommended for converting a company's standard specification into one suitable for an ECC contract.

1. Separate information into the Works Information, Site Information and information to be included in the Contract Data.
2. The second edition Guidance Notes give an extensive list of items to be covered in the Works Information on pages 21 to 23, which can be used as a checklist to ensure completeness. It is suggested that different items are placed in relevant sections of the Works Information which follow the general format of the nine sections within the ECC. For instance

- in subsection 1 of the Works Information, any information relating to communications and health and safety requirements are stated in the first section of the Works Information. In order to avoid any possible confusion, provide a clear statement of what the *Contractor* is or is not to do by the Completion Date for Completion to be achieved (see the first bullet point of clause 11.2 (13)). Where secondary Option L: Sectional Completion is used, this also needs to be considered for each section.
- in subsection 2, the *Contractor's* main responsibilities with regard to what he has to design and build, any procedures related to acceptance of the *Contractor's* design and the appointment of Subcontractors
- in subsection 3, any additional programming requirements (see section 3.1.2), the facilities and services to be provided by the *Employer* and *Contractor* and any reasons why the *Employer* may wish to use the works before Completion
- in subsection 4, procedures relating to testing and Defects. It is likely that the *Employer* or those preparing the specification on his behalf will want to develop more detailed procedures than those found in the core conditions for testing. Testing requirements are project and technology-specific which is why detailed procedures for these are not found within the ECC. Careful consideration is needed to ensure that the procedures give sufficient comfort to the *Employer* of 'fitness for purpose' versus placing onerous costs on both the *Employer* and *Contractor* (which ultimately the *Employer* will pay for). Particularly on multi-disciplinary projects, clear statements of different testing requirements for different types of work should be provided.
- in subsection 5, any requirements which affect payment
- in subsection 6, any additional information needed for compensation events and their assessment, although these are likely to be minimal
- any requirements relating to title (e.g. marking of Equipment, moving it in and out of the Working Areas

(clause 70)), insurance and disputes or termination in subsections 7, 8 and 9.

3. Do not 'hide' contractual and commercial information in the Works Information or Site Information. For instance, on one contract a statement to the effect that the *Contractor* would not receive payment for a completed activity until all the quality assurance documentation was complete was placed in the testing section. This information should either be in the relevant section of the Works Information or stated in the special conditions (Option Z) as appropriate. A danger of placing it in the Works or Site Information is that if it is not covered by the definitions within the contract, then it has no contractual significance.

4. Group similar information together, so that any ambiguities or inconsistencies can be identified and eliminated or reconciled. If information needs to be restated elsewhere in the documentation, then cross reference it back to one statement, rather than repeat it. This avoids the risk of ambiguity being introduced over time as people's personal foibles can tend to creep into the documentation. This might appear to go against the ECC's principle of avoiding cross referencing. However, the Site and Works Information should contain static information on the initial and final state of the *works*, whereas the ECC, to some extent, describes a dynamic process for the management of a contract.

5. Change references to the Engineer or Architect etc. to the *Project Manager* (for contractual and management issues) and to the *Supervisor* (for technical issues and acceptances). Be careful about referring to some commonly used documents which contain contractual entities who do not exist within the ECC. For instance, the term 'Engineer' in the Institution of Civil Engineers Arbitration Procedure (1983) or in standard specifications. If these documents are referred to in the Contract Data Part I, then the legal situation could be unclear.

6. Remove subjective phrases such as 'in the opinion of', 'to the satisfaction of', 'automatic' etc. and replace them with quantifiable measurements or objective criteria where possible. If the

Project Manager has to issue an instruction clarifying what is meant, then this is a compensation event under clause 60.1 (1), except in the two stated circumstances.

For physical conditions, boundary limits can be stated in Option Z. An example of this could be a stated assumption on the volume of soft spots to be found on site. It could be stated that soft spots are 10% plus or minus 2% of the total volume of earth that has to be moved in order to Provide the Works. If the *Contractor* has to remove less than 8% or more than 12% of the earth from the Site and replace it with suitable material, then the amount below the 8% or above the 12% becomes a compensation event. Alternatively, in a tunnelling contract, it could the tolerances on ground strata. The advantages of doing this at tender are stated by the second edition Guidance Notes on page 59: namely the assessment of risk by different Contractors at tender will be on a more common basis and reduced disputes during the contract.

7. The ECC does not include terms equivalent to Prime Cost Items or Provisional Sums. If those writing the Works Information are unsure about what is required, they should avoid imprecise descriptions, and seek to either state the requirements as a performance specification or to find out more information and produce a precise description. If neither of these is possible, then that component of the scope should be omitted from the Works Information, and a contingency included in the *Employer's* overall estimate for the project to cover the item.

One *Project Manager* with experience of two contracts reinforced the last two points by stating 'You have got to be positive . . . and not fuzzy on the technical requirements. You must be precise. The information to the *Contractor* must be complete'.

Because of the precision and tightness required in an ECC specification, a number of designers have estimated that it takes between 5 and 10% more time to prepare an ECC specification compared to a specification prepared for a traditional contract. This may well go against what was described by one interviewee as, 'the unacknowledged trend of getting less for less' from consultant designers. While this may mean the *Employer* has to spend more money prior to the contract being let, the designers interviewed felt that the process should produce a better and more buildable design, resulting in a reduced and more certain out turn cost.

National Power plc decided to completely rewrite their standard contract documentation observing many of the points outlined in the main text, placing a strong emphasis on clarity: using plain English, the same terminology as the ECC and having a consistent format. The documentation was updated by a multi-disciplinary panel, with the advantage that any text was rewritten in language which was comprehensible to all disciplines. The original 12 part specification was reduced to five parts.

- Part 1, Tender, which contains the conditions of contract and Contract Data Parts I & II, with any other commercial or contractual information contained in Option Z.
- Part 2, the General Works Information, which contains standards which apply across the whole organisation whatever the location of the work and that do not need to be changed for any contract.
- Part 3, the Specific Works Information, which provides the engineer writing it with a standard format.
- Part 4, the Site Information. This is rewritten in consultation between the head office contracts officer and individuals at the particular site, using the existing site information as a base. Once done for a particular site, only the contract-specific areas need to be revised for further contracts.

- Part 5, the Contract Schedules, which are pro-formas for bonds, parent company guarantees, safety plans, etc., and do not need to be changed for any contract.

Advantages found in practice were that

- the document is shorter and specific information is easier to find
- due to the modular nature of the ECC
  - o the commercial and contractual information can be assembled much faster than on a traditional contract form
  - o it is easier to write the technical specification and incorporate it to the inquiry document
  - o Site Information can be prepared by someone separate from the person preparing the Works Information.
- *Contractors*, who have bid on a number of contracts, now know where specific information is located in the document and find it is easier to identify differences from the previous contract. Therefore, the time spent preparing tenders is reduced.
- the amount of information returned to the *Employer* is substantially reduced, specific information can be located faster and differences from other tenders identified more easily, thus reducing the time spent evaluating them
- any mistakes found in the documentation from one contract can be more easily corrected in the documentation for the next one.

Lastly, the Guidance Notes suggest that the *Employer* should provide a summary of parts of the construction that the *Contractor* is to design, so that the *Contractor* is fully aware of his responsibilities and will not miss minor items situated in the main body of the Works Information. A number of *Contractors* complained that some items had inadvertently been left out of this summary, more by a lack of attention to detail than malice, but that this had affected their estimated profit margin.

In conclusion, while some fairly mechanistic changes are needed to change standard specifications into the ECC format, greater rigour and precision is also needed as the management processes within the ECC are more likely to highlight errors. There is value in training designers before they prepare specifications. This is likely to increase costs at the start of the contract, but should reduce construction costs. The long term benefits of converting to a standard format, modelled on the structure and principles of the ECC should be a saving of time in preparing the documentation, tender preparation by *Contractors* and tender evaluation and ultimately construction costs.

3.1.2 Specifying programme requirements

Tender programme

The *Employer* can ask for a programme with the *Contractor's* tender, which then becomes the Accepted Programme on signing of the contract. Just under half of the contracts in the research sample required a programme to be submitted with the *Contractor's* tender which was to become the Accepted Programme. However, none of the submitted programmes, in the *Project Managers'* opinion, satisfied the criteria in clause 31.3, and needed further development to do so. Therefore, they were taken out of the contract at the time of signing. Many *Contractors* (and some *Employers*) would also argue that it is unreasonable to expect too detailed a programme at tender, especially for operations starting late in the construction period.

Rather than requiring the *Contractor* to identify a programme in the Contract Data Part II, some *Employers* have asked, in the Instruction to Tenderers, for a programme capable of being developed into the Acceptable Programme and have specified the level of detail they require. The level required will vary with the size, value and complexity of the contract, but its purpose should be to give the *Employer* sufficient knowledge of how the *Contractor* intends to do the work for him, so that he is confident that the works will be completed to time and that the *Contractor* is not looking to play games.

As such it is suggested that it contains

- the starting date, *possession dates*, planned Completion and Completion Dates for any *section* of the works and the whole of the *works*
- dates when the *Employer* is to supply things such as acceptances, access, Plant and Materials or Equipment
- the critical path and float
- activities which correspond to those in the *activity schedule* (if using Options A or C), so that a cash flow forecast can be derived
- a general statement of how the *Contractor* proposes to do the work and a resource profile showing the general level of People and Equipment on site, as well as the presence of any specialist or expensive Equipment.

If the *Contractor* is incapable of supplying this information or submits a programme which is unrealistic, impracticable or unclear, then the *Employer* should consider whether to enter business with the *Contractor* or at the very least should enter into discussions with the *Contractor* prior to signing the contract. This might result in clarifications and adjustment to the programme and/or modifications to the Works Information prior to signing the contract which should be to everyone's advantage.

Accepted Programme
The ECC gives the *Employer* the opportunity to require the *Contractor* to show additional information to that required in clauses 31.2 and 32.1 e.g. highlight the critical path. If the contractual requirements of the ECC were more specific, then there is a danger that they could become a strait-jacket, imposing programming requirements which are unsuitable for the individual contract on

which it is being used. It is more appropriate for *Employers* to write any project-specific requirements in the Works Information.

While the ECC states what the programme is to show, it does not state how it is to be shown. Some *Employers* have specified that the programme will be prepared on certain software packages, with programme updates supplied on disk. Additionally, and some software can do this automatically, they have specified that changes from the last programme are highlighted. Furthermore, in order to avoid the programme becoming unwieldy, some *Employers* have specified a maximum allowable number of operations on the main programme, which can then be broken down into activities by the *Contractor* to ensure cash flow (section 3.2.2).

An aspect of good practice in programming is continual replanning throughout the contract. Multi-level planning is where, as the levels of uncertainty decrease and the time for an operation approaches, the programming is done in more detail by those more directly involved in the work.[*] The ECC is a major advance in terms of programming provisions over other forms of construction contract and does not preclude the programme becoming more detailed as the contract progresses. But it does not appear to encourage multi-level programming as an aspect of best practice and in this respect may be failing to promote good management. However, this is not to say it cannot accommodate it. On some contracts in the research sample, a short term programme, in addition to the main programme, was submitted, either voluntarily by the *Contractor* or specified in the Works Information. The outcome was a high level of co-operation and satisfaction with programming. The author suggests that potential users may wish to consider multi-level programming because

---

[*] See for instance:

- Laufer A., Tucker R. L., Shapira A. and Shenhar A. J. (1993). The multiplicity concept in construction planning. *Construction Management and Economics*, **11**, 1, 53–65.
- Faniran O. O., Oluwoye J. O. and Lenard D. (1994). Effective construction planning. *Construction Management and Economics*, **12**, 6, 485–499.

- method statements and resources for operations occurring in the distant future are likely to be less thoroughly thought through by the *Contractor* and/or scrutinised by the *Project Manager* than those for more immediate operations
- work in the distant future is subject to greater uncertainty and is more likely to change. Therefore, time spent preparing detailed method statements and resources is more likely to be wasted. On a number of contracts, the work content changed significantly between the start of the contract and the end.

For each level of programme, and it is unlikely that more than three levels will be needed for all but the most complex contracts, it is suggested that the *Employer* specifies the degree of detail, the format, the frequency of revision* and the planning horizon, with the idea that the greater the detail, the more frequent the revision and shorter the planning horizon.

An advantage of this is that when a compensation event occurs which affects the timing of the remaining work, only the programme appropriate to the size and impact of the compensation event need be updated. A potential disadvantage is that the extra complexity of different levels of programmes could result in even more work.

3.1.3 Completing Part I of the Contract Data

Part I of the Contract Data is the part which the *Employer* fills in. Information in the Contract Data is incorporated into the contract either by the use of *italics* (clause 11.1) or by direct reference. As such, the Contract Data Part I provides a means of further tailoring the contract strategy without the need for altering the terms and conditions in the main contract clauses. One *Project Manager* described it as a useful check list of issues which people should have thought about prior to putting a contract out to tender.

---

* The frequency of revision is stated in section 3 'Time' of the Contract Data Part I. The wording could be rewritten to say 'The *Contractor* submits revised <u>level 1</u> programmes at intervals no longer than . . .' and likewise for level 2 and 3 programmes.

A worked example of the Contract Data is supplied in Appendix 5 of the Guidance Notes. This section provides additional, and in some instances, considerably more detailed advice than is given in this Appendix or elsewhere in the Guidance Notes.

The first line of the Contract Data Part I states how the *Employer* implements his chosen contract strategy by stating the main and secondary options. It is worthwhile noting that the *Employer* must not choose more than one main option.

Authority and delegation

The Guidance Notes state that the *Project Manager* must be sufficiently close to the work and have time to carry out his work effectively. In a number of organisations, the named *Project Manager* has been a fairly senior person who has delegated his powers down to someone more involved with the day-to-day running of the contract. For instance, the engineer who prepared the documentation, be they an employee of the same company or an external consultant. Normally limits on changes to the Prices and the Completion Date that the delegated individual can agree have been specified. It is advisable that

- these limits are not set too low so that the delegated individual has very little power to agree issues and so has to constantly refer back to the *Project Manager*, thus undermining the delegatee's authority
- the delegated *Project Manager* has quick and ready access to the *Project Manager* at all times, so that the ECC's time scales for actions can be met
- the *Contractor* is informed of any limits on the delegated *Project Manager's* authority.

An advantage of the *Project Manager* being more remote from the contract is that he can perhaps think more strategically and dispassionately about it. For instance, how the individual contract fits in with other contracts which make up the project or in deciding on disagreements which might otherwise be referred straight to the *Adjudicator*.

It has been shown in practice that whoever is project managing the contract need not necessarily be physically close to the contract, but must be sufficiently involved and aware of what is happening on the contract. On smaller sites, the day-to-day management has often been delegated to the *Supervisor*, as the amount of work carried out on site has not warranted two people being present full time, with the *Project Manager* only being present for weekly meetings, periods of high activity or crisis. It is the author's opinion, based on experiences on some sites in the research sample, that the person given overall responsibility for delivery of the contract should be on site at least fortnightly, otherwise he will become too remote from the contract.

A number of contracts have been run from a head office several hundred miles from the Site. The named *Project Manager* delegated his day-to-day responsibilities to the *Supervisor* and kept in touch with both the *Contractor* and *Supervisor* by various means, such as video conferencing, telephone, E-Mail etc., as well as visiting the Site at least fortnightly. Both the *Project Manager* and *Supervisor* thought that this worked well in practice and the *Contractor* made favourable remarks on this arrangement. Indeed, he commented that the amount of communication between the *Project Manager* and the *Contractor* was unusually high.

Attitude

Another issue is what sort of people should the *Project Manager* and *Supervisor* be. Indeed, what sort of people should the *Employer*, *Contractor* and Subcontractor staff the site with? Interviewees from all sides of the industry were asked, in the light of their experience, what attitudes were desirable for people present on site on an ECC contract.

The following personal attributes were mentioned, with the most commonly mentioned given first: a willingness to change, trusting, open, team-minded, pro-active, communicative, honest, solution-orientated, commercially minded, fair, up front, systematic, realistic, ethical and able to negotiate amicably. The following attributes were given as undesirable attitudes: adversarial, confrontational, using the contract to make money, dishonest and procrastinating. Of note is the most commonly expressed attribute: a willingness to change. A number of more senior interviewees commented that the younger members of the staff team seemed both more willing and capable of changing.

If an *Employer*, having decided to use the ECC, wishes for a co-operative attitude to be established, then selecting a contractor with the above-mentioned desirable attitudes should be seriously considered. Some might wish to include attitude in their selection process for the *Contractor*. One senior member of a *Contractor's* staff noted that many of his contemporaries, who are deemed to be good at their jobs, are traditionally confrontational and, in his opinion, not suitable to oversee an ECC job. Similarly, companies participating in an ECC contract, whether *Employer*, *Contractor*, Subcontractor or consultant, would be wise to select personnel with the desirable attitudes mentioned above. The author is aware that this was positively undertaken on a number of sites within the research sample.

The selection procedure on one contract involved pre-qualification from which six *Contractors* were selected to bid in the normal manner. Each *Contractor* whose priced bid was within 10% of the lowest, was then invited to an interview with the *Employer's* site team where the *Contractor's* proposed site team was evaluated on attitude and how well the two teams could work together. Selecting the *Contractor* partly on attitude and people is quite common when entering a partnering type arrangement.

Skills

General skills, or prerequisites to individual skills, that were mentioned as being desirable for the top people on site, whether they represented the *Contractor* or *Employer* were (with the most commonly mentioned given first) more: pro-active/forward looking, commercially aware, professional, experienced and competent. A number of interviewees commented that the *Project Manager* and *Contractor's* agents need to be better all round managers than on conventional non-ECC contracts as they have to have an appreciation of the cost and time implications of their decisions, rather than just technical issues. This is because they can no longer make their technical decisions in a vacuum, leaving the time and cost consequences to be fought over by the claims consultants and quantity surveyors at the end of the contract. However, on the larger sites, they will be advised by others e.g. planners, quantity surveyors and technical experts.

It could be argued, as a number of individuals in the research sample did, that under the more traditional conditions of contract, the programme is seen as a reactive tool to support claims while, under the ECC, it is a more pro-active tool for forward planning of the works. This implies a change in emphasis in people's skills. Thirty percent of interviewees in the research specifically stated that increased planning skills, as opposed to progress 'loggers', were desirable on ECC sites compared with other conditions of contract.

In a similar vein, 15% of interviewees noted that increased estimating skills were needed on site, as opposed to claims type quantity surveying skills. A number of interviewees stated that estimating required a change from just using a bill of quantities and dayworks with time calculated records to a greater use of operational/resource-based estimating, where costs are assembled more from first principles. Consequently, quantity surveyors involved in estimating need a greater appreciation of programming, even though they may not be doing it themselves. A quote from a *Contractor's* agent illustrates the point:

> most surveyors do not do estimating. They are used to . . . doing it
> retrospectively, when they know what all the costs are and can

compile everything . . . . The danger for them, under the ECC when they are compiling it in advance, is that they have forgotten something. The fact that you have to build into that quote any potential extension of time and other knock on effects . . . means that, at times, you have to be quite cute to pick it all up.

A *Contractor's* chief quantity surveyor made similar comments. On his site, not only were there more quantity surveyors and planners on site than there would have been for a non-ECC contract, but personnel were moved on and off the site depending on whether they could adapt their attitude and skills to those required of the ECC. They found that planners and estimators who were used to working from a full specification tended to require information that was not always available and were too methodical and therefore too slow. They found that staff who had site experience and were willing to, in his words 'take a view on a matter' were most appropriate. A frustration on his site was that the *Employer's* quantity surveyors also did not have these skills and outlook. For example, they tended to insist that construction costs arising from compensation events had to be justified in full from first principles, regardless of the expense involved in calculating the minutiae versus the sums involved. This led to additional costs for both parties.

In the same way that the principal people on site have to be more competent, a number of *Employers, Contractors* and Subcontractors assigned their more capable staff to the early NEC contracts. One interviewee went so far to as to state that the ECC 'demands that every contract is staffed up with competent people'. This suggests that the industry-wide adoption of the ECC could force up standards of professionalism in the construction and engineering industries. Some interviewees raised the wider point that while planning and estimating skills were present in the construction industry, they are not common enough and that this has training implications.

> One Subcontractor's managing director stated that
>
> the calibre of people we needed on the job was at the top end of the range, because administratively you have got to get it right — there is no scope for you getting it wrong, for muddling through . . . . That meant the job has got done in the right way and I think one thing the ECC is going to do is make us more professional . . . . I think a lot of the people in the industry, who maybe ought not to be there, are not going to find a hiding place . . . . We learnt very quickly on this job that if we were not professional, it would hurt us.

Selecting the Adjudicator

The primary requirement for the adjudication procedure to operate is for an *Adjudicator* to be selected. The second requirement for it to work effectively is that all parties have trust in the *Adjudicator's* independence and competence, so that his decisions are respected and the likelihood of a dispute being taken further is decreased. The research found that

- when no *Adjudicator* was suggested by the *Employer*, the likelihood of one being appointed by the Contract Date was reduced. Indeed, on two contracts, the parties were 'squabbling' over the name of the *Adjudicator* when neither had any intention of using him. The result was that an Adjudicator was never appointed.
- when only one name was suggested by the *Employer*, *Contractors* often did not query or object to the choice of the *Adjudicator*, despite in some cases apprehension about him, in case it was perceived as being confrontational and would count against them.
- the highest degree of satisfaction with the selection procedure was when three or more names were suggested, from which the *Contractor* could pick one.

However, Employers who let a large number of contracts under the ECC (or indeed under any form in the UK since the introduction of the Housing Grants, Construction and Regeneration Act (1996)) would have a large number of Adjudicators on their books who, hopefully, will have little to do. Consequently, some have specified that an Adjudicator is only appointed if a dispute arises. This has the advantage that the *Adjudicator* can be selected for his specialist knowledge which relates to the matter in dispute and, if it becomes necessary to pay retainers to Adjudicators, reduced corporate overheads. Potential problems with this approach are that the *Adjudicator* has a very limited time to become familiar with the contract and the appointment of the *Adjudicator* can become contentious in itself, as different Adjudicators like arbitrators attract reputations. Further, as on one contract within the research sample, the appointment of the Adjudicator could be seen by the *Contractor* as a barrier, put in place by the *Employer*, to be overcome before going to adjudication.

The Guidance Notes suggest qualities that are desirable in an *Adjudicator* (page 77 of the second edition). A number of *Employers* deliberately put forward names of ex-contractor personnel with experience in the technical aspects of the construction who they felt would be both competent and fair. This nullified potential objections from *Contractors* that the *Employer* was choosing someone who would just see things from their own perspective. In the UK, because of the introduction of the Housing Grants, Construction and Regeneration Act (1996), many institutions now have a list of trained Adjudicators and, when asked, should be able to select quickly one with the appropriate contractual, and industry background from a database.

Concluding, it is suggested that a number of names are put forward by the *Employer*, that these names are taken from an institution's adjudicator's list, that the individuals have the personal qualities and knowledge stated in the Guidance Notes and that they have experience in the technology of the contract and, lastly, that they are familiar with the ECC conditions.

Period for reply

It is suggested that the *period for reply* specified is not longer than two weeks. On relatively simple contracts, where for instance there is little or no *Contractor* design, there is no good reason for it to be greater than a week. It may be appropriate to specify different *periods of reply* for different issues e.g. three working days for enquiries for further substantiation for compensation events and two weeks for acceptance of the particulars of the *Contractor's* design.

Time for submission of first programme and intervals for revised programmes

It is suggested that, if possible, the time given for the *Contractor* to submit his first programme for acceptance is not more than the difference between the Contract Date and the date when the *Contractor* is given possession of the site i.e. a programme is submitted by the time the *Contractor* is mobilised and on site as this is when change starts to occur. If a programme is not in place, then it is hard to evaluate the time and cost consequences for all but the smallest of changes under the ECC. If multi-level planning is adopted (section 3.1.2), then different time periods may be specified for different levels of programme.

It is also suggested that the *assessment interval* for payment is a multiple of the interval for submitting revised programmes, particularly when Options A or C are being used as the programme will then tie in with the *activity schedule*, and monitoring and payment become one procedure.

Testing and Defects

It must be remembered that the number of weeks stated for the *defects date* is the equivalent of the maintenance period in other contracts, while the *defects correction period* is the time that the *Contractor* has to correct Defects that exist or become apparent after Completion once they are notified. In some cases, it may be appropriate to specify quite a long *defects date*. For instance, on a new road or road renewal project, it might be worthwhile specifying a time scale in which the road should not deteriorate from normal use. It may also be worthwhile specifying different *defects correction periods* for different types of work or situations. For instance, if a certain piece of machinery in a new factory breaks down, then the whole factory may close down until it is fixed in which case a *defects correction period* of a day for production machinery may be appropriate, while for other aspects a more appropriate period may be two weeks. Where safety is compromised, again, a shorter *defects correction period* may be appropriate.

The assessment interval

Some *Employers* have agreed with their *Contractors* to specify this as four or five weeks in order to fit in with the accountancy systems, with *Employers* being billed on, for example, the last Friday of each month. Others have used the term 'monthly'.

Weather

It is strongly recommended that the place where the weather is to be recorded is the Site or quite close to it. On some of the contracts in the research sample, this did not happen and the *weather measurements* were taken at a distant meteorological station at which the *weather data* was recorded.* While this provides a very clear cut test for a compensation event, the site was firstly having to wait until the end of the month plus a week to be supplied with the *weather measurements* and secondly, it sometimes had nothing to do with the weather actually encountered on site! For a contract over six months duration, it is probably cheaper to set up a simple weather station on site and to compare these *weather measurements* with the *weather data* supplied by the meteorological centre. Providing the weather encountered on the site and at the existing meteorological station are historically comparable, the important thing, in the author's opinion, is the clear cut nature of the test compared with the 'exceptionally adverse' weather test of other non-ECC contracts.

---

* The *weather measurements* which occur during the period of the contract are compared with *weather data* taken from existing meteorological stations. If the *weather measurements* exceed a value which occurs less frequently than once in ten years, then this is a compensation event.

Employers should only consider specifying additional weather measurements when they affect the work on site. Alternatively, an additional compensation event can be specified in the Contract Data Part I. When doing so, they should ensure that what is being measured is what will affect the work.

One project involved raising the level of a road bridge over a small river. This river was prone to flash flooding due to weather conditions encountered upstream and not in the near vicinity of the Site, which in turn flooded the road. When flash flooding occurred, work would not only have to stop, but could also involve reconstructing some of the temporary works. The *Contractor* noted that this was not a physical condition that 'an experienced contractor would have judged . . . to have such a small chance of occurring' (clause 60.1 (12)) nor was it a weather compensation event (clause 60.1 (13)). As it was an uncontrollable risk, the *Contractor* thought that the *Employer* should, at the very least, have taken some of the risk for it occurring by specifying a threshold at which the river height became a compensation event. This would have resulted in a cheaper tender Price.

On work being done at sea from a barge, the *Employer* initially tried to define an additional weather compensation event as wave height, but because of difficulties in measuring wave height, this was derived from wind speed. Both *Contractors* pointed out that swells can come in from storms out at sea several days after a storm had passed the geographical location of the Site. It was subsequently agreed that an additional compensation event would simply be when they were unable to work at sea and this work was on the critical path.

Form of tribunal
The Guidance Notes provide ample advice should the *Employer* wish to specify arbitration as the tribunal procedure. However, some *Employers* now wish to go straight to the courts, because should a party not like the outcome of an arbitration, they can, in certain circumstances and jurisdictions, appeal to the courts. Further, as a process for gaining justice, the use of litigation and the courts may not be more expensive and time consuming than arbitration on complex disputes.

Some *Employers* may wish to specify a series of alternative dispute resolution procedures before resorting to arbitration or litigation. This is known as a dispute ladder and starts with amicable settlements and extends to the courts. The amicable settlements could be conciliation or an executive tribunal, where an independent chair and an executive from each of the parties, who have not been directly involved in the contract, put aside a day to hear the facts of each party's case. They then make a decision which is acceptable to both sides bearing in mind the circumstances. If that decision proves unacceptable to one of the parties, they then proceed to the next ladder of the dispute process. If all these steps fail, it is only then that they proceed to arbitration or litigation. Some *Employers* and *Contractors* may even wish to agree some form of rapid and amicable dispute resolution procedure prior to notifying a matter to Adjudication.

Additional compensation events
Employers should only add additional compensation events when they affect the work on site and when doing so, should ensure that what is being measured is what will affect the work. See above comments on weather in this section.

Employers should give considerable thought before deleting a compensation event. They certainly should not delete a compensation event over which they have predominant control or responsibility i.e. Compensation events 60.1 (1) to (11) and 60.1 (14) to (18). For physical conditions and weather compensation events (60.1 (12) and (13)), the *Employer* will be paying a premium to the *Contractor* if he places this risk on the *Contractor*. As Contractors are generally more risk averse than Employers (as their profit margins are less), it is likely that the *Employer* will pay more in the long term for allocating an uncontrollable risk to the *Contractor*. Generally the less information the *Contractor* has on this risk, the less he will be able to structure his work in order to minimise the likelihood of occurrence and the impact of it on the work, so the greater the premium required for taking that risk. As an absolute rule, risk should not be allocated to a party unable to sustain the consequences of that risk.

The Contractor's share percentages and share ranges (Options C and D) Detailed explanation of the operation of these clauses is given in the Guidance Notes. Less detailed is the advice on setting the share formulae. Similar factors need to be considered as for selecting the main and secondary objectives. The principal considerations are

- the project objectives and the degree of certainty that the *Employer* wants over these
- the contract constraints
- the ability of the each party to influence Actual Costs and risks, both in reducing costs and the potential for overrun
- the ability of each party to withstand the consequences of a risk occurring and Actual Cost escalating
- market conditions
- the interaction with other incentives.

Research in America has found that positive incentives are more effective than negative ones[*] i.e. bonuses are preferable to damages. This stands to reason as if the Employer wants exceptional performance, then the targets need to be set to motivate the Contractor (and himself) to achieve excellence. Negative incentives, which are

---

[*] Ashley D. B. and Workman B. W. (April 1986). *Incentives in construction contracts, Construction Industry Institute Source Document 8.* Construction Industry Institute, Austin, Texas.

generally applied if mediocre performance is not achieved, by contrast set the target level of performance at just above mediocrity.

While it is reasonable to suggest that the *Contractor* should suffer should the contract overrun its target, if the *share percentage* is too punitive then the *Contractor* is likely to cease co-operating and start fighting the *Employer* rather than the problems which are causing the overrun. This may impinge on the contract's other objectives. Further information and guidance on the working of target cost contracts is given in CIRIA Report 85.[*] Updating and expanding this work and the investigation of other contractual incentive mechanisms are also the subject of a current research project by the author.

3.1.4 Other issues

Supply of a bill of quantities when using activity schedule options
An issue which *Employers* may wish to consider is whether to supply a bill of quantities to tenderers, without prejudice and separate from the formal contract documentation, for contracts let under the activity schedule options. This is now suggested in the second edition Guidance Notes. It does have its dangers!

On all the Option A contracts that the author researched, where the *works* had been substantially designed prior to award, the tendering *Contractors* have used a bill of quantities for estimating. This is because quantity is a component of cost. However, the bill of quantities has not been supplied by the *Employer*, but prepared by the individual *Contractors* or by a quantity surveying firm commissioned jointly by them.

Interviewees, with experience of ECC contracts, have put forward the following arguments for the supply of a bill of quantities by the *Employer* under Option A or C.

---

[*] Perry J. G., Thompson P. A. and Wright M. (1982). *Target and cost reimbursable construction contracts*. CIRIA Report 85. Construction Industry Research and Information Association, London.

- It allows the *Contractor's* estimator to determine quickly the resource needed to prepare the tender.
- Even if using the operational method of estimating i.e. working out costs from first principles, the estimator still has to determine the quantities which make up each activity as quantity is a component of cost.
- Having the total of the quantities allows a check of the calculations.
- Without it the estimator has to start from a blank sheet, so the process of taking off quantities is slower than it would be when purely checking the quantities.

Interestingly, none of the interviewees put forward arguments on the grounds of tradition or because of the use of estimating databases. The above factors suggest that the time available to the *Contractor* for actual estimating will be less and, because there is no built in check on quantities, the estimate may be less accurate — one *Contractor* thought that preparing a full bill of quantities himself added about 40% to his tendering costs, although other *Contractors* have not put the figure as high as this. As the ECC becomes widely adopted, it may lead to an increase in Contractors' overheads which, due to the duplication of effort in taking off quantities, *Employers* will ultimately pay for.

Another reason put forward for the preparation of bills of quantities by the *Employer* is that many minor errors in the specification are picked up in the process. On one contract, the *Employer's* quantity surveyor, despite favouring the use of activity schedules, noted that many minor compensation events arose from changes to the Works Information (clause 60.1 (1)), which he thought would normally have been picked up in the preparation of a bill of quantities. However, there is a good argument that the bill of quantities need not be prepared to the level of detail or format of the current industry standards — e.g. CESMM3 and SMM7 — as their purpose is different under the ECC.

For these reasons, it seems sensible that *Employers* supply a bill of quantities of some sort to tendering *Contractors* which are separate from the contract documentation and not referenced in them, even if it is only a list of principal quantities supplied as an Appendix to the Instructions to Tenderers. However, some lawyers would undoubtedly argue that whatever disclaimers are put on them, *Contractors* would still be able to come back at the *Employer* if they can show that the quantities were material to them submitting a given Price. Two possible ways around this objection exist.

- *Employers* give their best estimates of quantities, but specify tolerances on the accuracy e.g. plus or minus 5%, with the stated tolerance reflecting the degree of confidence in the estimate.
- *Employers* give the contract documents to a firm of quantity surveyors a month or so before the contract is let, so that they can identify any errors which could be corrected. This firm of quantity surveyors could then sell the bill of quantities onto the tendering *Contractors*.

Seminar

Prior to or at the same time as issuing the tender documentation, some *Employers* have held half-day training sessions to the pre-selected tenderers. At this, as well as outlining the technical nature of the job, they have given an overview of the ECC and explained how it differs from traditional contracts and why they are using it, emphasising the principal changes needed in practice and culture. During the presentation, they have stressed that it is their interpretation of the ECC and that it is in the *Contractor's* interests to receive further and independent training. The fact that the *Employer* has taken the trouble to brief the *Contractors* has been well received by them and taken as a sign of good faith and commitment.

Assessing tenders

The criteria for assessing *Contractor's* tenders should be stated in the Instructions to Tenderers. In the ECC, this needs to include calculating the potential effect of the various percentages returned in Part II of the Contract Data. This is examined in detail in section 3.3.1.

3.2 PREPARING THE TENDER

The principal differences to conventional contracts in preparing a tender under the ECC are

- accuracy
- programme and activity schedules
- understanding the Schedule of Cost Components (SCC)
- filling in the Contract Data Part II.

3.2.1 Accuracy

Numerous *Project Managers*, *Contractors* and quantity surveyors acting on their behalf, have stated in the light of their experiences that it is much harder 'to make up' for a low tender under the ECC. This is for a number of reasons.

- The regularly updated programme, which includes resources and method statements, means that the original costs and time scales are more transparent.
- The contemporaneous assessment of compensation events prevents the *Contractor* waiting until the end of the contract, doing a cost/expenditure reconciliation and claiming an inflated amount from the *Employer* in expectation of receiving considerably less — the 'rule of thirds' as one *Employer* referred to it.
- The rigour of the whole compensation event procedure, including the use of the Schedule of Cost Components, which gives headings for which the *Contractor* can charge additional sums, means that the justification for additional costs is more rigorous and transparent.

As one *Contractor's* contracts manager stated 'you can play the same games under the NEC, but you have to be a lot cleverer to play them, the rewards for playing them are less and, in playing them, you are working against the ethos of the contract'. Asked what the consequences of being found out were, he replied that 'you would probably get less payment and at a later date. Consequently, I do not think it is worth playing them'. The implication is that *Contractors* need to have greater confidence in the accuracy of their tender and, in order to have this, need to apply greater rigour to its preparation.

For *Employers*, an advantage is that the tender Price will be more realistic and closer to the out-turn cost, which will aid his financial projections and budgeting.

3.2.2 Programme and the activity schedule

The contractual sanctions for not having an Accepted Programme were outlined in section 1.4.4, and suggestions for the *Employer* specifying more precisely how he wanted the Accepted Programme were presented in section 3.1.2.

Under Option A, the priced contract with activity schedule, payment is linked to completion of activities specified in the *activity schedule*. It is essential, therefore, for the items listed in the *activity schedule* to correspond with the operations in the Accepted Programme. A benefit of this is that monitoring and payment become one and the same procedure as the *Contractor* is paid for completing an activity/operation. Under Option C, the target contract with activity schedule, the *Contractor* is paid Actual Cost plus the Fee and, during the contract, planned expenditure can be compared to actual expenditure as a means of evaluating progress. Under both options, the allocation of a sum to an activity which accurately represents the true costs of doing that work aids the assessment of the change in costs due to any compensation event. As one *Contractor's* quantity surveyor stated 'Evaluation at tender stage . . . is different, because you have to think in terms of the *activity schedule*; . . . you have to really think about preparing the programme at tender time, rather than necessarily when the contract is awarded'.

When tendering under an activity schedule option, the *Contractor* needs to establish the main activities and their quantities from the programme. Therefore, he needs to prepare a programme in sufficient detail for him to do this. Having derived the main activities and their quantities, some longer duration activities will need to be further split into smaller activities to ensure cash flow. Especially under Option A, the priced contract, *Contractors* should ensure that

- all the work that is in the Works Information is included in the *activity schedules*, otherwise they will not be paid for it (under Option C, the target will be artificially low).
- each activity is clearly identifiable, so that there is a minimum of discussion over whether the activity is complete and hence the *Contractor's* entitlement to payment. This means avoiding subjective phrases such as the term 'first fit' which is traditionally used on building projects for mechanical and electrical work.
- operations of a long duration are subdivided into shorter activities. However, some long duration operations do not lend themselves easily to subdivision as there is no clear cut off point. Specifying set percentages of the operation as activities may be appropriate.
- finishing operations are separated from the associated main operation. For instance, on a tunnelling contract, the *Contractor* may wish to divide the tunnel into segments, each of which has additional activities such as pointing, fitting the wedge block keys, initial clean, repair of defects and final clean.
- Subcontractors' activities mesh with their own.
- delivery of major items of Plant and Materials to site are specified as an activity when they will not promptly become part of the *works*.

However, some dangers of over extensive sub-divisions of *activity schedules* are

- under Options A and C, the *Contractor* has to show the start and finish of each activity on the programme submitted for acceptance. Therefore if each activity is a bar on a programme, then the Accepted Programme can become over complicated and, as a consequence, hard to follow and unwieldy. This has been a common problem.
- under all Options, the *Contractor* has to show order and timings of operations and statements of method and resources for each operation in the programme. If each activity is an 'operation', it therefore requires an individual method statement and resource

schedule (due to clause 31.2 of the ECC), which can create a great deal of paper work.

- the simplicity is lost and there tends to be a reversion towards the bill of quantities where everything is measured.

For these reasons, it is suggested that, conceptually, an operation is made up of activities as this will lead to fewer statements of method and resources. It also lends itself to the concept of multi-level programming (see section 3.1.2) where the operations are shown in the highest level programme and activities in the lower ones. If the *Contractor* is submitting the programme in electronic format, then it may simply be a matter of double-clicking on an 'operation' bar, which then expands out to show the 'activities' which make up that operation.

When evaluating tenders, *Employers* or their representatives should also bear these points in mind. For instance, asking for simplification of the *activity schedule* on award. However, *Employers* should resist the temptation of specifying activities, and thereby affecting when the *Contractor* will receive money. If they do, then the consequences might be that

- the *Contractor* will alter his programme to optimise his cash flow rather than the construction process. The author is aware that this happens on other forms of contract where the Employer specifies milestones, or
- the *activity schedule* will not mesh with the Accepted Programme, because all the *Contractor's* operations are not in the *activity schedule* proposed by the *Employer*.

The danger of the *Employer* dividing the work up into segments which do not match how the *Contractor* will do the work also applies to bills of quantities. This was identified on one contract within the research sample and has consistently been highlighted in research reports as a problem under any form of contract.[*]

[*] See, for example: NPWC/NBCC Joint Working Party (1990). *No dispute: strategies for improvement in the Australian building and construction industry*. National Public Works Conference, Australia.

120

On one contract, the *Project Manager* did specify the activities for which the *Contractor* would receive payment. These did not match how the *Contractor* intended to carry out the work and he distributed the costs of miscellaneous and unspecified operations across various activities. Consequently, the Accepted Programme contained resources and method statements for operations which did not relate to the activities in the *activity schedule*. Although it is the change in resources from those in the Accepted Programme that should be used to assess the financial affects of compensation events, this led to severe problems in establishing the base costs when evaluating compensation events. The *Project Manager* stated that in future he would let the *Contractor* specify the activities.

On another contract, the *Employer* went part way towards this, asking for activities to be grouped under broad headings for tender comparison purposes. The tenderers replied that they had some activities which did not fit into any of the headings specified by the *Employer*. After some discussion, a 'miscellaneous' heading was introduced.

3.2.3 *Understanding the Schedule of Cost Components (SCC)*

In the ECC changes in Actual Costs, due to compensation events, are calculated by evaluating the change in method from the original method in the Accepted Programme. From this, the change in resources stated in the Accepted Programme are derived. Apart from Option F, the management contract, to satisfy the definition of Actual Cost, the generic cost heading of the resource has to be listed in the Schedule of Cost Components. Once understood, the SCC has helped in assembling and agreeing costs compared with the procedures (or lack of) in traditional contracts. However, a frequent comment from personnel on both sides of the industry is that, with hindsight, they failed to understand or appreciate the importance at tender of the quoted percentages which are applied in the SCC when assessing a compensation event arises. These are tendered by the *Contractor* in Part II of the Contract Data. Failure to understand the purpose and use of these percentages at the tender evaluation stage can, and has, led to the calculated Actual Costs (what the *Employer* pays to the *Contractor* ignoring the *fee percentage* when a compensation event occurs) being higher than the real cost to the *Contractor*. In a few cases, the difference has been excessive. Unfortunately, how cost is built up in the SCC does not always reflect how cost is built up in practice and this is explored in this section.

There are two Schedules of Cost Components — the Schedule of Cost Components (referred to hereafter as the normal SCC) and the Shorter Schedule of Cost Components (referred to as the shorter SCC). If the *Contractor* is assessing a quotation, the normal SCC is used unless it is agreed to use the shorter schedule. If the *Project Manager* is assessing the quotation for reasons stated in the contract (see clauses 64.1 and 64.2), then he can use the shorter SCC (clause 63.11).

The other use of the normal SCC is under the cost-based contracts (Options C, D and E), where the *Contractor* is reimbursed his costs plus a percentage Fee. To be an allowable cost for which he can be reimbursed i.e. Actual Cost, the item has to be listed in the normal SCC or be a payment made to a Subcontractor.

3.2.3.1 *The (normal) Schedule of Cost Components*
People   The three bullet points listed in the second edition of the ECC state the criteria for people that can be included in calculations for Actual Costs. Under these three bullet points, the costs of any employee of the *Contractor* who is not paid according the time worked on site and is on site less than a week, are not counted as Actual Cost. On smaller sites, planners and more senior personnel sometimes visit the site on a weekly basis, so their additional time due to a

compensation event cannot be charged. Provided there are no major changes in scope which necessitate more of their time on site, then this does not cause a problem. If more of their time has been required on site, *Contractors* have asked for additional payment for these peoples' time, which has sometimes caused argument. It may therefore be worthwhile for the parties to agree how much commitment, on a monthly basis, of more senior personnel is allowed for in the *Contractor's* tender and to agree a monetary sum per additional hour or half-day for their services. This means if there is a large number of compensation events or a big one, then their experience and input is given willingly, rather than grudgingly, to aid the reduction of costs and/or time as reimbursement of their costs will be guaranteed.

Under the normal method, the cost of people is worked out from first principles allowing for all the factors listed in **People 1**: 11, 12 and 13 and an hourly or daily figure for each category of person can be determined.

Equipment The author would not recommend working out *Contractor*-owned Equipment by the normal SCC as it is fraught with difficulties. In theory it uses straight line depreciation where the *Contractor* is reimbursed the cost of depreciation for the time used plus a percentage — the percentage for Equipment depreciation and maintenance — applied to this sum. This percentage is tendered by the *Contractor*. The research identified seven problems with the method, ranging from misleading terminology to difficulties in agreeing the actual purchase price or first cost and average working life and the fact that the site is charged hire rates by their internal hire company regardless of how cost is worked out under the method. Even if the *Contractor* quotes depreciation and mainte-nance for special Equipment, there are still difficulties in working out first cost. Consequently, it is recommended that for specialist or large Equipment, the *Contractor* quotes a rate using the Short Method.

An alternative, especially when a rate has not been quoted at tender, could be that the rates that the site, as a cost centre, is paying for Equipment which falls into one of the three categories listed in Equipment 22, are at competitive open market prices. If the *Contractor* cannot demonstrate this then the *Project Manager* is entitled to make an assessment of the rate.

Under the normal SCC, the cost of externally hired Equipment would be the hire rate, plus consumable and transport, the latter related to transporting the Equipment to and from the Working Areas. It has some advantages over the shorter SCC for externally hired Equipment: namely, when Equipment is working 24 hours a day or if the *Project Manager* suspects that the *Contractor's* percentage for adjustment for listed Equipment (given in the shorter SCC) is too high. Its disadvantage is ease of use as hire charges and cost of consumables have to be checked.

Plant and Materials   The costs listed in the normal SCC are reimbursed at cost provided, as with all Actual Costs, they are 'at open market or competitively tendered prices with all discounts, rebates and taxes which can be recovered deducted' (clause 52.1).

Charges   Additional costs for items in Charges 41, 42 and 43 are charged at cost. When there is a compensation event, the items listed in Charges 44 are covered by a percentage — the percentage for Working Area overheads — which is applied to the cost of People. However, there is a problem with this approach in that it covers both 'provision and use'. The *Contractor* is therefore faced with a dilemma. Should he

- assume that there will be no change to the Completion Date due to a compensation event and allow for extra use only in the percentage for Working Area overheads
- allow for all time-related costs in the percentage as well as additional usage, but run the risk that when the effect of the various tendered percentages is assessed for tender comparison purposes (section 3.3.1), he will have priced himself out of contention, or
- put in a percentage which is somewhere between these two extremes.

Which option he chooses will, to some extent, depend on the nature of the job e.g. the likelihood of different risks occurring and whether it is a project with a time deadline. However, there is still an element of a gambling, as the *Contractor* has to foresee the extent of compensation events and to what extent they will lead to delays in the Completion Date.

A literal reading of the contract would mean that, under the target cost and cost reimbursable options, this percentage is still applied to the cost of People. This goes against the concept of reimbursing the *Contractor* his costs and undermines one of the principal benefits of cost-based contracts: namely transparency. A consequence may be that *Contractors* try to maximise 'People' Actual Costs and minimise what they spend under Charges 44.

As a result of these criticisms, the author would recommend that some of the more major costs under Charges 44 become reimbursed at cost, rather than be included in the percentage for Working Area overheads. Further, from discussions with *Contractors*, it would seem to more closely correlate with how they incur costs if this percentage was applied to their preliminaries rather than People costs. If this was done, then the percentage would effectively become a round up percentage for minor fixed and time-related costs and for use-related costs e.g. the fixed cost of installing a telephone, the time-related rental charges and use-related cost of both the number of phone calls made and, say, wear and tear on cabins etc.

Another alternative, adopted by one *Employer*, is for the *Contractor* to give his time and use-related costs per week at tender as part of the make up of the Prices. If the Completion Date is delayed, the Prices are adjusted by this rate multiplied by the additional time on site due to a compensation event. A danger of this is that the rate does not match the *Contractor's* true costs, either by design i.e. he anticipates that the contract duration will be extended and therefore loads the time-related rate, or accident. In the latter case, it does not aid transparency of costs.

Manufacture and fabrication, and Design   Both of these headings require the *Contractor* to submit hourly rates for various categories of

125

employee for work that is carried out off site. A tendered percentage for factory or design office overheads is applied to these rates. It is suggested that the *Contractor* is allowed to submit different rates and percentages for different factories or design centres or for different types of work, rather than one set of rates and a percentage.

3.2.3.2 Shorter Schedule of Cost Components

People   The same comments that were made on the normal SCC about *Contractor's* staff who are on site for less that a week apply to the shorter SCC.

Under the shorter SCC, people costs are worked out from first principles, but items 12 (e) and (f) and 13 (a) to (n) in the normal SCC are included in the percentage for people overheads.

Equipment   In the shorter SCC, the *Contractor* puts forward a published list of Equipment, such as the Federation of Civil Engineering Contractors' rates, [*] and then tenders a percentage for adjustment to the rates listed in the schedule. This percentage has been generally been calculated by

- working out the cost of hiring and operating five or six of the most common pieces of Equipment present on site from first principles
- comparing the figure arrived at with the stated published list
- working out the average difference to gain a percentage.

This percentage is usually negative, but depends on such factors as site location and access, state of the economy etc. For specialist Equipment or Equipment where costs are large, it is advisable for the *Contractor* to give special rates for 'other Equipment'. In doing so, the *Contractor* should state and the *Employer* should clarify if unsure, exactly what is included in the rate.

---

[*] Since July 1998, the FCEC schedule has been replaced by the CICA (Civil Engineering Contractors Association) schedule. When comparing tenders, it needs to be checked to which schedule the percentage adjustment is applied.

Plant and Materials costs are calculated in the same way as in the normal SCC.

Charges The *Contractor* tenders a percentage for people overheads which is applied to the sum of People costs worked out under **People** in the shorter SCC. This has to cover all the items listed under **Charges** in the shorter schedule and people costs items 12 (e) and (f) and 13 (a) to (n) in the normal SCC. A similar problem exists as for the percentage for Working Area overheads in the normal SCC: that is should he allow for additional usage only in his percentage, additional usage and time or somewhere in between. It could be argued that the problem is greater under the shorter SCC as more is included in the percentage. This problem perhaps accounts for the wide discrepancies in the level of tendered percentages that the author has seen for people overheads ranging from 40% up to 300%!

If the adjustments, suggested by the author, to the operation of **Charges** in the normal SCC are made, then it is suggested that *Contractors'* concerns about recovering their fixed and time-related charges will be reduced. The shorter SCC, which can only be used by agreement or when the *Project Manager* is assessing a compensation event, can then be used when there is no delay to the Completion Date. It therefore only has to cover the additional usage costs of preliminaries as most, if not all, of the people costs items 12 (e) and (f) and 13 (a) to (n) in the normal SCC would not be encountered. This would make it much easier for *Contractors* to assess and tender realistic and consistent percentages.

Manufacture and fabrication, and Design The same comments apply for these as in the normal schedule.

3.2.4 Filling in Part II of the Contract Data

The determination of the percentages, which are tendered in Part II of the Contract Data, has been given in the previous section.

The *Contractor* has to state the names, experiences and qualifications of the key people he intends to use on the contract. The same comments which apply to the selection of the *Employer's* key people (section 3.1.3), also apply to the selection of the *Contractor's* key people.

The fee percentage

Two problems with the *fee percentage* emerged during the course of the research.

- A lack of understanding of what the *fee percentage* covers, leading to a wide variation in the tendered percentages.
- Containing the Subcontractors' *fee percentages* within the main *Contractor's fee percentage*, as the main *Contractor's fee percentage* is applied to Actual Costs, regardless of whether the work is subcontracted (under Options A and B). Therefore, if the Subcontractor's *fee percentage* is greater than the *Contractor's*, the latter will lose money on compensation events.

The *fee percentage* covers everything that is not stated in the Schedule of Cost Components. This is effectively the *Contractor's* off-site overheads, insurances and bonds and profit. *Contractors*, it is suggested, should be aware of what proportion of their costs are made up of off-site overheads. If they are not, then this should be calculated prior to tendering on the ECC. As a guideline, the average off-site overheads

- of a medium to large construction company are between 6 and 8%. *Contractors* who had tendered less and subsequently won the contract found that they were losing money on compensation events. As a result, they were trying to push up Actual Cost which caused friction at site level.
- for a typical small building company with an annual turnover of approximately one million pounds per annum, the off-site overheads may be 15%.
- for a small specialist subcontractor, the off-site overheads may be 25% and, in some cases, their tendered *fee percentages* have been as high as 40%.

This is logical as the larger the company, the greater the likely economies of scale and thus the lower the percentage overhead. Additionally, the smaller the value of work being conducted on site, the more likely it is that the *Contractor's* management and administrative staff are responsible for a number of sites, which they visit on a weekly basis. Therefore, their costs cannot be included in People costs when assessing compensation events, so they are counted as off-site costs, which increases the *fee percentage* further.

The fact that the smaller the company, the higher the off-site overheads, and hence the *fee percentage*, raises a problem for a main *Contractor* tendering under the ECC, as he is likely to have to accommodate Subcontractor's *fee percentages* which are higher than his own. If he pushes up his own *fee percentage*, then his bid may become uncompetitive. If he does not, then he risks losing substantial sums of money if he wins the contract. The problem is aggravated by *Contractors* only receiving the Subcontractor's tender documents and associated *fee percentages* a few days before their tender bid is due.

Unfortunately, there is no perfect way around this problem for *Contractors*, short of *Employers* and, in the future, the NEC Panel modifying the ECC. However, to mitigate the effects, main *Contractors* could ask for their principal Subcontractors to tender the *fee percentage* and the percentages that are tendered in Part II of the Contract Data early in the tender period. Additionally, some of the costs in the individual Subcontractors' *fee percentage* can be moved to, for instance, the percentage for Working Area overheads, the percentage for people overheads and/or the percentage for manufacture or fabrication overheads. If done excessively though, this undermines both the concept of transparency of cost which leads to co-operation and the idea behind the SCC: namely, that it more accurately reflects how Contractors costs are incurred than, for example, the bill of quantities model.

Where different companies and therefore sites are to be used for off-site manufacture and fabrication and for off-site design, *Contractors* may wish to state different percentages for different locations in order to avoid the danger of paying more to a Subcontractor than they receive under the main contract.

3.3 EVALUATING THE TENDER

3.3.1 Evaluating the effect of the tendered percentages

The principal difference for the *Employer*, when assessing *Contractors'* tenders under the ECC compared with traditional conditions of contract, is calculating the effect that the various percentages returned in Part II of the Contract Data would have should a certain value of compensation events occur. On contracts where this was not done, there is some evidence that the percentages tendered have been excessive.

A model tender assessment sheet is given in Appendix 4 of the Guidance Notes (for use with Options A and B). It is suggested that *Employers* use this as a base to develop their own tender assessment sheet. The *Employer* has to make certain assumptions about the amount of change that is likely to occur in the contract. Depending on which percentages will be used to assess compensation events, the *Employer* has to make estimates of how much of a particular resource will be used. This means that, for a fully auditable process as is necessary in the public sector, *Employers* need to

- decide on a monetary sum for the on-site cost of compensation events, which is then
  - split into a ratio which reflects the expected extent that the normal and shorter SCC will be used
  - split into a ratio for each of these two figures which reflects the expected proportions that Equipment, People, and Plant and Materials will be used on compensation events. For civil engineering work, a starting point could be 35:25:40. However, this would vary with the type of work e.g. a pure earth moving contract would have no Plant and Materials.
- estimate how many off-site people hours are likely to be used in design and for manufacture and fabrication.

These figures can then be multiplied with the relevant percentages and rates tendered by the *Contractor* and added together to give a sum which is then multiplied by the *fee percentage*. This gives a sum for additional costs due to compensation events. When this is added to the tendered total of the Prices, a monetary sum is gained for a *Contractor's* tender which can be compared with others for the purposes of tender evaluation leading to the award of the contract.

The author is aware that some *Employers* consider the above process too formalised, with its credibility reliant on 'guestimates' which may well not materialise once the contract is let. Instead, they look closely at the individual percentages and rates which the *Contractor* has tendered. They can gain insight into how the *Contractor* has priced the work and how his costs are built up. By comparing the percentages and rates with those of other *Contractors* (both with those tendering on the same contract and with previous ones), the *Employer* can identify extreme rates which may lead to ill feeling during the contract. This could be because

- the percentages which the *Contractor* has submitted are too low and he is therefore losing money on every compensation event. He therefore tries to push up his forecast level of resources used and/or their costs per unit prior to applying the percentages to them.
- the percentages which the *Contractor* has submitted are too high. The *Project Manager*, aware that the *Employer* is paying over the odds, tries to push down the forecast level of resources used and/ or their costs per unit prior to applying the percentages to them, or
- the percentages are unbalanced leading to the *Contractor* always proposing, for instance, Equipment-dominated solutions to compensation events if he has a good percentage adjustment for listed Equipment compared to the percentage for people overheads.

All the above have happened to varying degrees on some sites with adverse affects on relationships. It is suggested that any extreme values of percentages should be openly addressed during the pre-contract negotiation phase.

The question is often asked why people cannot tender daywork rates for people. The answer is they can and some *Employers* have asked for daywork rates for particular categories of workers. However, the principle is that the *Contractor* is paid his costs plus an allowance for profit which is in the *fee percentage*. If daywork rates, or for that matter, rates in the bills of quantities are used to assess compensation events, then it is less likely that his true costs are reimbursed. In some cases this will be to the *Contractor's* benefit and in others to the *Employer's*. It is argued by the author that mismatches between how costs are incurred and how the *Contractor* is reimbursed are partly responsible for the adversarial atmosphere which often exists under traditional conditions of contract. The use of daywork rates can perpetuate this atmosphere.

3.3.2 Other issues

Other issues which the *Employer* may wish to include for in the tender assessment process are

- an analysis of the submitted programme to ensure its realism, practicality and completeness. This could lead to further questions in order to clarify the *Contractor's* intentions.
- an adjustment to the total used for comparing tenders (i.e. the sum arrived at through the process outlined above) by taking account of the time value of money. For instance, if it is costing an *Employer* £5000 per week not to have the asset in use, then the £5000 could be subtracted from a *Contractor's* tender for each week that Completion is shown to be ahead of the Completion Date. An additional factor to bear in mind is the amount of free float shown in between operations off the critical path as it is to the *Contractor's* advantage to place float as a time risk allowance (section 3.4.2).
- a cash flow analysis. For contracts tendered under the activity schedule options, this is comparatively easy as the Prices for each activity which will be completed in a certain month can be summed. For other options it is not so easy.
- an analysis to take account of the time value of money. The sums arrived at in a cash flow analysis can be discounted back or forward to a set date using a pre-agreed discount percentage.

- the *Contractor's* design. This can be assessed, for example, on architectural merit in the case of a building or the technical solution in the case of some process plant. Following any discussions, it is important to confirm what aspects of his design and what commitments are to be incorporated into the contract by referencing them in the Contract Data Part II under the *Contractor's* Works Information. Failure to do this does not tie the *Contractor* to fulfilling his proposals or what was agreed.

- the key people involved. The type of people that it is desirable to have on site was discussed in section 3.1.3. The qualifications and experience of the key people put forward by the *Contractor* can be analysed. In a few cases, *Employers* have told the *Contractor* that a certain individual is not appropriate due to previous experience with that individual. Other *Employers* have used face-to-face meetings and structured interview evaluation techniques to assess the *Contractor's* site team and to include it as part of the tendering procedure. This is very much in line with selection procedures used at the start of partnering arrangements.

Target cost contracts
Under target contracts, the assessment procedures described above are just as relevant. However, in target cost contracts, an analysis should also be conducted for potential saving and overruns on the adjusted Prices. The Price for Work Done to Date is Actual Cost with the *fee percentage* applied to it. On some contracts, especially those run with a partnering agreement, some savings on Actual Cost can be expected. For more riskier work, where the risk is not defined as a compensation event, Actual Cost may rise. In the latter case, if the *Contractor* tenders a high *fee percentage*, then the effects of any cost overrun will be exaggerated and could undermine any incentive for the *Contractor* to reduce costs. These sort of scenarios should be addressed when setting the share ranges and percentages (see also section 1.3.1.3).

3.4 POST AWARD

This section describes the principal steps necessary after the award of the contract i.e. the Contract Date, but prior to mobilisation on site i.e. the first *possession date*. The principal issues which need to be addressed are

- training for those involved in the running of the contract
- development of the programme by the *Contractor* and, if possible, acceptance of the programme by the *Project Manager*
- the development of a system of pro-formas and logging system for contractual communications.

It was suggested by a number of interviewees that a week or two extra should be programmed into the project programme to allow for these issues to be addressed, especially for those new to the ECC.

3.4.1 Training

The importance of skills and attitude has been stressed in sections 1.5.3 and 3.1.3. The most important attitude was highlighted as a willingness to change. However, people have to know what to change to. They also have to know what they have to do and preferably why. Indeed, the why is possibly the most important factor because it gives people the motivation to change. Hence the need for training. As one project participant, who had not had training on the then NEC, admitted 'If you just pick up the NEC and read it and don't have any training on it, then . . . you probably miss the whole point of it' or as a senior project manager put it 'It's just plain different. It means that people who have been scienced in other forms have got something else to learn'.

A number of training organisations now offer training on the ECC. While the ECC is a legal document, it is also, as many observers have noted, almost a manual for project management. This suggests that purely legally-based training, in the traditional style of training on contracts, is not completely appropriate. Secondly, to gain the most from the ECC involves cultural change and, to some extent, skills change. Again, it is suggested that training which does not put this over and concentrates purely on the mechanics of operation is also lacking. Potential participants should bear this in mind when selecting the training organisation and the individual trainer.

Having explained the why and given an overview of how the contract works, the author has received extremely positive feedback from workshops designed to tease out the more important (and sometimes contentious) aspects of the ECC. In so doing, participants gain insight into how the ECC can help them achieve their objectives, lose their fear of the contract, and, while not knowing all the answers, know where to look and how to find them. Often these training workshops have been jointly funded and attended by both the *Employer's* and *Contractor's* personnel. This aids team building as issues are brought out into the open.

3.4.2 Programme

This sections builds on the advice given in sections 3.1.2 and 3.2.2. The author previously outlined the concept of multi-level planning, where there is continual re-planning throughout the contract, involving different levels of personnel as the time for the operation approaches and levels of uncertainty decrease. The first stage of this is developing the programme submitted at tender into a programme capable of acceptance. It is suggested that this is a joint effort between the planner who assembled the tender programme, the planner who will be involved in the job, and the *Contractor's* agent. On small jobs, the last two may be one and the same person. Any comments by the *Employer/Project Manager* on the tender programme should be considered. At the same time, the people who will actually be supervising and directing the work (e.g. foremen and section engineers) should be developing the initial short term programmes and statements of methods and resources for each operation. Once the contract is won, it is advisable to develop the programmes on software which satisfies the requirements both of the ECC and any criteria stated by the *Employer* in the Works Information. Research in the early 1980s indicated that the availability of programming software on site pays for itself.* With the reduction in costs of personal computers and programming software and the frequency of revision of programmes under the ECC, the benefits will be even larger now.

Once the programmes have been developed, they should be submitted to the *Project Manager* for acceptance. They will almost inevitably not be to the *Project Manager's* complete satisfaction and it is in the *Contractor's* interests to know this sooner, rather than close to end of the first *assessment interval*, otherwise he may have a quarter of the Price for Work Done to Date retained from the first assessment (clause 50.3). Equally, once the *Project Manager* has accepted that a programme shows all the information stated in clause 31.2, he loses this powerful sanction.

As a result of the *Project Manager's* rejection on specified grounds (clause 31.3), the *Contractor* will need to modify the programme. It is important that the *Project Manager's* comments are given in a constructive manner, noting the exact reasons upon which it is rejected and, ideally, what the *Contractor* needs to do to make it acceptable. The detailed critique has been done either through a written report or face-to-face discussions.

On two of the 29 contracts researched, the sanction to retain money from the first assessment was used. Because of the manner in which the parties approached the contract and each other, this did not cause any lasting damage to relations. On three of the contracts, money was not retained when it could have been, either as a result of the *Project Manager* not going through the submitted programme with sufficient rigour or through fear of being seen as adversarial. This

* Reiss G. (1992). *Project management demystified — today's tools and techniques.* E & F N Spon.

caused problems later in the contract in the assessment of compensation events, which did result in friction between the parties.

As well as examining submitted programmes to ensure that the *Contractor* is complying with the requirements of the contract and Works Information, it is suggested that the *Project Manager* also views the programme assessment as a means by which he can contribute positively to progress and reducing costs. For instance, on one site the *Contractor* was required to put a service main through the perimeter fence of an operational site. The Works Information stated that the *Contractor* had to erect a temporary security fence, take down part of the permanent fence, place the service through the gap and then reinstate the permanent fence before dismantling the temporary fence. This was shown as a week-long operation on the Accepted Programme. The *Project Manager* asked whether the *Contractor* could dismantle the permanent fence, put the service main through, and reinstate the fence within a day, thus saving the erection and dismantling of the temporary fence. The *Employer* would supply a security guard for the day. The answer came back that by working a long day with additional men, they could. Even though this was let under Option A, the priced contract with activity schedule, the savings were split, so both parties gained.

3.4.3 Communications

The research found that it was an almost universal opinion that more contractual communications occurred during the implementation phase of an NEC/ECC contract as issues were dealt with contemporaneously. However, opinion was divided on whether overall there was more or less paper work from the *starting date* to the settlement of the final account compared with other conditions of contract. The following principles are put forward for guidance on setting up procedures for effective communication, while minimising unnecessary paperwork. These are drawn from best practice communicated to the author during the research, namely

- discuss and agree things orally. Confirm them in writing.
- create an environment conducive for verbal communication
- have fortnightly meetings, so that all issues are resolved within the specified time scales
- have a structured system of pro-formas
- have a system for logging in the various communications and the time for their responses
- ensure these pro-formas and systems include Subcontractors
- be aware that there will be more communication than with traditional contract forms and have the above in place prior to the start of the contract.

On the majority of sites, much of the communication is verbal, as information can be exchanged and decisions or agreement arrived at much faster than through writing letters. However, verbal communication is not contractually valid, as it is not 'in a form which can be read, copied and recorded' (clause 13.1). As one contract participant stated, 'notifications should just be merely backing up what you have agreed by talking to each other'. The overriding principle is: *discuss and agree things orally, confirm and summarise in writing*.

Communication on a personnel level can be encouraged by such things as partnering workshops and team-building days. The openness 'kick-started' by these events can be reinforced and sustained partly by the physical environment. For instance, on some contracts the offices of the parties were deliberately sited in the same building or set up adjacent to each other. Where possible, this included the principal Subcontractors' offices. Various *Project Managers* and *Contractors* operated an 'open door' policy. On other contracts, the *Supervisor* worked alongside the *Contractor* on an almost hourly basis. On one contract, the *Project Manager's* office was located directly opposite the *Contractor's* site agents, the *Supervisor's* opposite the *Contractor's* chief engineer and the same applied to the planners and quantity surveyors offices etc., rather than being at the far end of opposite corridors. There was an understanding that if a door was closed then access was restricted, but this was a rare situation and normally a fully open door policy operated.

On one contract, partly to ensure that decisions were made on small items and partly to impose a discipline on his construction managers of agreeing things to a time scale, the *Project Manager* set up fortnightly meetings to clear minor early warnings, technical queries and compensation events in addition to the normal progress, quality and safety meetings. The author is aware that this *Employer* has written a procedure into the contract to make these 'wrap-up' meetings a contractual obligation.

On all but one site researched, a system of pro-formas was used. The most common system evolved with use, but basically consisted of six forms, namely

- a technical enquiry sheet, with four classifications on it: technical enquiry/resolution, alternative proposal, notification of a possible compensation event and notification of early warning
- a *Contractor's* submission sheet, which could be used for the submission of drawings, programmes, compensation event quotations and notice of tests etc.
- a *Project Manager's* instruction sheet, with three classifications on it: general instruction, instruction changing the Works Information and a proposal to change the Works Information
- a compensation event sheet, which confirms the time and cost effects of a compensation event and whether or not to proceed
- a *Supervisor's* sheet for notifying the *Contractor* that an inspection is to be done, or the results of that test or to record the discovery of a Defect or an instruction to search
- a *Contractor's* sheet for notifying the *Supervisor* that an inspection is to be done, the results of that test or the discovery of a Defect.

This system avoided writing long letters, with each party trying to include contractual terms to suggest or refute a later claim. Instead, participants noted that more agreed information was communicated and communication was more focussed on the solution. Sample pro-formas, derived from this system, are given in Appendix 1. It is, however, recommended that these are used as a base and that they are tailored to individual companies and projects.

> One *Contractor* commented that, as a result of this system, their site management team probably spent half as much time writing contractual letters to the other party as they would have on a traditional contract. Instead they were able to concentrate on programming and working with the *Project Manager* to save time and/or money. Partly as a result of this, on each of the jobs the *Contractor* was involved in, his profit margin steadily increased as the contract progressed. However, the author is aware of one *Employer* who has close to 30 different pro-formas, which as a system they admitted is quite unwieldy. The author is also aware of one *Employer* who abandoned the use of the ECC because of 'administrative problems'. The lesson is clear: devote time pre-contract to setting up an administrative system, as it will save you time during the contract.

The pro-formas need to have continuity and a procedure is needed to keep track of the various stages of communications. On the majority of contracts this was a log kept in a book. On one, it was kept on computer, while on another the whole communication system was computerised. On one large contract, a full time administrator was employed by both parties to keep track of communications and ensure each organisation responded within the time scales specified in the ECC. An issue to consider when devising the pro-forma system is that of relating one communication to previous ones, in order to create an audit trail should the need arise to refer to previous communications.

If the communication system does not extend down to include Subcontractors, then the *Contractor* may be putting himself at risk due to a Subcontractor's action or default. It is therefore in the *Contractor's* interests to educate Subcontractors and make them conform to the contract and its time scales. All contractual communications between the *Employer's* designers or specialists and Subcontractors have to be routed through the *Project Manager* and *Contractor*.

On three contracts within the research sample, technical discussions were held directly between the *Employer's* designers and the works contractors under the *Contractor*. The *Contractor* and *Project Manager* were then informed of the technical decision, with the latter confirming its implementation contractually by using the pro-formas. On one contract, the *Employer's* designers and Subcontractors were communicating directly, often without the *Contractor's* knowledge. This sometimes resulted in small savings in direct costs being outweighed by delay and disruption costs when the *Project Manager* authorised the change without consulting the *Contractor*. Control of unnecessary change is a crucial aspect of good project management.

On a number of sites, personnel admitted that, with hindsight, they had not given the above issues enough consideration prior to work beginning on site. They were therefore having to put them in place rapidly and without due consideration, which often resulted in later modification. The time spent doing this affected the management of the physical work. In the words of a *Project Manager*, under an ECC contract, 'you need to hit the ground with your feet running, because where you get hit hardest is in the early stages'.

3.5 CONSTRUCTION PHASE

If the steps outlined in the previous sections have been followed, many of the problems typically found by first time users of the ECC should be reduced. It is then a question of refining procedures and gaining familiarisation with the conditions of contract. The vast majority of users interviewed in the research found the ECC as easy or easier to use than traditional forms after only one contract. However, there are still some new processes and ways of working under the ECC that need to be carefully thought about and learned. A critical issue is the manner in which compensation events are assessed. This and other changes needed in the construction phase are discussed below.

3.5.1 Payment

The exact operation of the payment provisions will depend on whether the work is in England and Wales, in which case it will be subject to the provisions of the Housing Grants, Construction and Regeneration Act (1996). The main provisions of Act also apply in Scotland and Northern Ireland, albeit with some minor changes in detail. The NEC Panel have drawn up alternative clauses which comply with the Act. If ordering a new copy of the ECC, these should come with the order. Otherwise, the alternative clauses can be obtained without charge from Thomas Telford Publishing.

In the unaltered clauses, the *Project Manager* has one week from the assessment date to certify the payment (clause 51.1). The *Project Manager* considers any application for payment which the *Contractor* has submitted on or before the assessment date (clause 50.4). In reality, all *Contractors* in the research submitted details of the amount they considered they were due. Despite this, the author is aware that some *Employers* have written in an additional clause making it mandatory for *Contractors* to submit details in order to avoid items being missed out of assessments. The *Project Manager* gives details of how the amount due has been assessed (clause 50.4) and if he is late in certifying the amount then interest is paid on the amount which he should have certified until he does certify the amount (clause 51.4). This is so that the *Contractor* can plan his cash flow. A result of the one week certification period, particularly on Option B, the priced contract with bill of quantities, is that those acting on the *Project Manager's* behalf have tended to measure completed work as the month progresses, rather than in the period in between the assessment and certification dates. This avoids a week of intense activity to agree the monthly measure.

Unless stated in the Contract Data, the *Contractor* is paid within three weeks of the assessment date, which should be a minimum of two weeks after the certification. In some *Employer* companies, this may mean speeding up the administrative procedures relating to payment, otherwise the *Contractor* will be entitled to interest on the late payment.

Under the alternative clauses designed to satisfy the Housing Grants, Construction and Regeneration Act (1996), the *Contractor* may still submit to the *Project Manager* an application for payment before the assessment date and the *Project Manager* still has to certify the amount due by the 'date due' — a week in the ECC. Again, if he does not do so, interest is paid on this amount until he does so. The *Employer* has to pay the *Contractor* by the 'final date for payment' — three weeks from the 'date due' (not the assessment date), otherwise interest is paid on the late payment. If the *Employer* intends to withhold payment, he has to inform the *Contractor*, with reasons by the 'prescribed period' — seven days in the ECC — before the 'final date for payment'. If the *Employer* does not follow this procedure and withholds payment without informing the *Contractor*, or the *Contractor* successfully overturns the *Employer's* decision through Adjudication, then the *Contractor* can give seven days notice of his intention to suspend performance. This right ceases as soon as payment is made. In the ECC, the *Contractor* is entitled to the additional time and cost of suspending performance which is assessed as a compensation event. The assessment would include any demobilisation and remobilisation costs, as well as the length of time that work was suspended.

3.5.2 Early warnings

All the *Contractors* interviewed adopted the principle of early warning as a matter of policy in order to avoid subsequent assessments of compensation events being reduced (clause 63.4). Indeed, the early warning procedure was often over-used in the early stages of a contract with the *Project Manager* finding himself almost swamped with early warning notifications for every minor matter which could possibly result in a compensation event. After a discussion, the threshold for early warning normally settled down to a workable level. However, the importance of early warnings should not be diminished. The need to early warn should be driven into the minds of site personnel.

The words in the contract seem to imply that an early warning meeting is a formal affair (clauses 16.2 and 16.3). In fact, it could just as easily be a meeting out on site or an informal meeting in one of the participant's office. While there might only have been one or two formal early warning meetings on most of the sites researched, less formal ones were a weekly, if not daily, occurrence on many sites. The system of proformas should recognise this. As mentioned in the section on communications (section 3.4.3), one *Project Manager* would have fortnightly early warning meetings to wrap up and resolve minor early warnings. Under the ECC, the *Project Manager* records the outcome of these meetings and gives a copy to the *Contractor* (clause 16.4).

An example of the impact of the early warning procedure was illustrated on a tunnelling contract. While sinking the shaft, the parties found that they had hit a layer of chalk which contained flint. Initially, they decided to increase the jacking force and therefore the number of jacks. However, the flints were at the level that the tunnelling machine was meant to start boring at and it was not designed to go through flints, so a decision was made to deepen the shaft and start the drive three metres below the original level. Within two days, the *Employer* had committed an extra £750,000 to the project. However, both parties believed that they had probably saved around £3 million compared to starting the tunnel at the original level. Despite the contract being let under Option C, the target contract with activity schedule, and the existence of a partnering agreement, all parties thought it unlikely that they would have made that decision, and certainly not as rapidly, without the early warning procedure being specified in the contract.

3.5.3 Agreeing the time and cost effect of minor compensation events and updating the programme

In an ideal world, the time and cost effects of every compensation event would be agreed prior to the work proceeding. Wherever this is possible, this should be the aim (see section 3.5.4). However, it is not always practicable for small to medium compensation events as

- the work would have to stop while the compensation event was evaluated and agreed, leading to lots of small delays in addition to those arising directly from the compensation event. Completion and hence the Completion Date would be affected adversely.
- by the terms of the contract, 'if the programme for the remaining work is affected by the compensation event, the *Contractor*

includes a revised programme in his quotation showing the effect' (clause 62.2). As virtually all compensation events will affect remaining work to some extent, this implies that new programmes would be an every day occurrence, imposing an unnecessarily heavy administrative load on those attempting to operate the contract.

In reality, on all the contracts within the research sample, the procedure for evaluating the time effects of minor compensation events evolved to adopt the following form, namely

- it was agreed that the event was a compensation event
- the work proceeded so as not to delay the progress of the *works*
- the additional people and Equipment hours were recorded together with any additional Plant and Materials used
- Actual Costs plus the Fee were assigned to these direct costs and submitted within the three week period for quotations
- before a new programme was assembled by the *Contractor* and submitted for acceptance, the *Project Manager* and *Contractor* would meet to agree the cumulative effect of minor compensation events, in terms of disruption to other work, and overall delay to Completion. These effects — and the effects of delays for which the *Contractor* was responsible under the contract — were then shown on the revised programme, which having had input to, the *Project Manager* usually accepted on the first submission.
- Actual Costs plus Fee were assigned to these indirect costs and submitted within the three week period for quotations.

This procedure does not provide the *Employer* and *Contractor* time and cost certainty at any point in the construction as the authors of the ECC would like. It is, however, a significant improvement on the traditional 'claim' for delay and disruption, which is usually submitted several months after construction is complete under traditional contracts. This provides no basis for the effective project management of the contract. The ECC procedure does have the advantage of creating a rolling final account, an up-to-date estimate of when Completion will be achieved and, because the Completion

Date is constantly visible, all parties know where they stand and what they are aiming at.

Agreement on the effect of variations/compensation events is also easier as the people involved in the assessment

- are using a more up-to-date programme which has more information in it and has been previously accepted
- are based on site and the work is relatively recent. This compares to the traditional claim being developed by 'claims consultants' etc. who have become involved months if not years after the event happened and are trying to reconstruct reality second hand, usually based on partially incomplete records.
- are discussing disagreements in time scales of days or at worst a week or two, rather than weeks and months as can happen on traditional forms when assessment is delayed until at the end of the contract.

Another issue which has caused problems, particularly on building sites, where many of the Subcontractors are small organisations, is that they simply lack the sophistication and motivation to price compensation events using the Schedule of Cost Components, but are quite happy to work using bill rates. Pragmatism is needed here — if the *Project Manager* or those representing him are happy with the rate and the compensation event is of a fairly minor value with little or no impact on the overall programme, then the work involved in evaluating the change in Actual Costs can be made using rates in the *bill of quantities* rather than using the Schedule of Cost Components. If the main contract is let under an activity schedule option and the *Contractor* has prepared his own bill of quantities for use with the Subcontractors, then these can be used in order to save time.

3.5.4 A methodology for agreeing the cost of major compensation events

Section 3.5.3 discussed methods of agreeing the time effects of minor compensation events. This section puts the case for the prior assessment of more major compensation events and gives a methodology for agreeing the cost effects of them in a rational and constructive manner. This methodology should reduce the sometimes contentious atmosphere engendered when agreeing costs.

Under traditional conditions of contract, *Contractors* generally like to have additional work assessed retrospectively using records. This is because

- they are risk averse
- daywork rates normally more than cover the cost of labour and construction plant.

Under the NEC/ECC, a distinguishing feature of *Contractors* who achieved final profit margins more than they had expected at tender was their willingness to price work in advance of it proceeding. While this is not always practical, some made a conscious effort to prioritise the assessment and agreement of work not yet done.

The benefits to the *Contractor* of doing this is that it gives him the incentive to manage the works efficiently so that he can make profit over and above that in the Fee. *Employers* gain three benefits, namely

- in order to gain early agreement, *Contractors* submit more realistic Prices. This results in less management time being wasted going through and agreeing the quotation.
- once the changes in Prices and the Completion Date are agreed, the *Contractor* is no longer motivated to make the most of the *Employer's* misfortune
- Price and time certainty.

The extent to which these benefits can be realised depend on how willing the *Contractor* and *Project Manager* are to assess and agree compensation events where the physical work has not yet been done. One *Contractor* prioritised the assessment of compensation events where the work has not yet been done over that done on records. The *Project Manager* also prioritised the assessment of these quotations over those using records. This collaborative approach gave both parties the benefits outlined above.

The following is an attempt to formalise an approach which evolved informally on some projects for the assessment of compensation events. It is suggested that the parties agree, in order

- the cause of the compensation event
- the desired outcome or range of outcomes and any constraints on how it is to be achieved
- any assumptions in the above
- any additional risks, an approximate estimate of their impact and likelihood of occurrence, resulting in a decision on who takes them
- the required change in the *Contractor's* method of working. From this the changes in the resources directly involved in the activity can be determined.
- the change, if any, to the overall duration of the contract
- the change in Actual Costs related to each of the last three points
- communication and iteration.

Lastly, some other tips are given to aid the agreement of compensation events.

The author is aware that this might seem a little idealistic. It is however based on observation of real contracts where agreement has been reached rapidly and it has been critiqued and improved with suggestions by practitioners. It also involves a change in attitude from both parties administering the contract: namely, that the *Contractor* is entitled to fair recompense and additional time when a compensation event occurs providing he can justify it with *sufficient* rigour and the *Contractor* does not try to take excessive advantage of the situation when a compensation event occurs.

The cause of the compensation event

The main reason for spending a little time determining the cause of the compensation event is that it is sensible to define and analyse the cause of the problem, rather than rush into a possibly inappropriate solution. Another reason is that any cost and delay associated with the compensation event can be placed in a category corresponding to the sub-clause number in clause 60.1. At the end of the contract, the *Employer* can see under what headings he has spent additional money and/or had Completion delayed. He can then take steps to improve his performance on the next contract, progressively increasing the price and time certainty in which his projects are delivered, as well as decreasing their out-turn price. For compensation events under clause 60.1 (1), the authors suggest a further sub-division for changes in the Works Information to distinguish between *Employer* generated changes (e.g. changes in scope) and those that originate from the design organisation (e.g. poor quality specifications).

The desired outcome and any constraints

A number of *Contractors* interviewed complained that, under traditional conditions of contract, too often the *Employer* or his representative give inadequate descriptions or instructions of what is required from the *Contractor* for variations. It was thought that this is because they themselves did not know what they want and hoped that the *Contractor* would come up with something suitable. This then results in argument when it does not conform to their idea of what is suitable. This has also been experienced on some contracts let under the NEC/ECC. If the *Project Manager* wants accurate quotations in advance of the work proceeding, then it is a matter of common sense that he supplies the *Contractor* with precise information on which to base that quotation.

It should be noted that specifying the desired outcome or range of outcomes is not the same as specifying the solution. Defining the problem is the start point, specifying the outcome is the end point and a solution is the way to achieve the outcome. Under the ECC, the *Project Manager* could ask for quotations with a least time outcome or least cost outcome. He could ask for quotations to reach a desired outcome through a range of technical solutions. If the Parties are really working in a spirit of mutual trust and co-operation, then the *Project Manager* could even give the *Contractor* the cost that the quotation must not exceed and ask for the best value outcome that can be achieved for the money. Constraints restrict the solutions that can be applied to achieve an outcome and the *Project Manager* should state these up front in order to avoid abortive work by the *Contractor*.

Assumptions
An activity which has not yet been performed will, in all likelihood, contain some uncertainty. The *Contractor* is allowed to include for cost and time risk allowances which are at his risk under the contract in his quotation (see clause 63.5). Guidance on this is given in the next part of this section. Some uncertainty, however, arises if 'the effects of a compensation event are too uncertain to be forecast reasonably'. These uncertain effects need to be identified and formulated as assumptions in accordance with clause 61.6. Failure to do so or to do so with sufficient precision can result in

- the assumption being found to be wrong resulting in an additional compensation event (clause 60.1 (17)), or
- the *Contractor* putting a large margin in his quotation to cover the uncertainty. The *Project Manager*, alarmed at the time and/or cost impact, redefines the assumptions and the *Contractor* has to requote.

As one *Employer's* quantity surveyor stated:

> There are a given set of circumstances which can be made into assumptions when requesting a quotation. These make it very difficult for the *Contractor* when there are other things which we may have not stated as assumptions, because he then has to make his own assumptions. Now that could inflate a quotation . . . . We have to reach some agreement as to what is and is not included.

One frustrated *Contractor* in the research sample made the point that he had better things to do than churn out quotations which, on the basis of past experience, were going to being chucked into the bin and redone.

If an assumption is too uncertain for the *Contractor* to price it rigorously, it is sensible for effort to be spent reducing the uncertainty or, to put it more bluntly, if the *Project Manager* wants accurate and realistic quotations, he must give the *Contractor* detailed and accurate information on which to base that quotation. However, there will be situations where the *Contractor*, in assembling the quotation, finds that he is making assumptions about assumptions! In these cases, the author suggests clarification is sought from the *Project*

Manager. This will avoid proceeding with the quotation and placing a large cost in the quotation to cover the uncertainty. This can only cause acrimony when the *Project Manager* assesses it as effectively it means that the detailed work involved in preparing the quotation becomes abortive, resulting in reworking the quotation for it to be accepted. See also the section 'Other tips'.

On one contract which predominantly involved earth moving, the *Employer* failed to gain planning permission for a temporary dumping area in time. The *Project Manager* asked for three quotations based on different assumptions, namely

- the contract was terminated (the ECC has more extensive termination clauses compared with other contracts making termination a viable option without becoming embroiled in legal disputes)
- the earth moving continued through the winter months
- the *Contractor* stopped work over winter and remobilised at the start of the next earth moving season.

After some negotiation the third option was chosen as the most favourable. In the words of the *Employer's* contracts officer 'it was the first time, in my experience, that we have really been able to make a proper project management decision based on good information'. Asked what would have happened under traditional conditions of contract, his reply was 'we would have probably carried on with the work regardless (i.e. over the winter) and had a bun fight at the end of the contract'. This sentiment was echoed by others within the research sample in the light of their experiences. For the more major compensation events, both those representing the *Contractor* and *Employer* thought that the process of pre-assessment and negotiation ultimately saved the *Employer* money as what was desired was more defined by the *Project Manager* and more efficiently implemented by the *Contractor*.

Risks
The idea of the *Contractor* taking on additional risk once the contract is let is an anathema to many contractors. Similarly, the consideration of risk from the *Contractor's* viewpoint is a new experience to many who represent the *Employer* on construction contracts. On some contracts within the research sample, it was an area with which participants did struggle. On others, *Contractors* accepted and priced for construction risks in compensation event quotations with the *Project Manager's* knowledge and approval. They then used their expertise to minimise the impact of these risks on the construction programme and costs, which they otherwise would not be motivated to do.

Conceptually, the management of risk has three phases, namely

- identification of possible risks
- analysis to establish the likelihood of occurrence and potential impact should they occur
- the development of strategies for the management of the more major and frequently occurring risks.

Various levels of sophistication were observed in the research in the approach to the management of risk.

At one extreme, *Contractors* would try to add a standard percentage to the Actual Costs of all compensation events. No specific risks would be identified for a specific situation and, consequently, no action to reduce the impact or avoid it altogether would be taken. Within the research sample, agreement on the level at which this percentage should be set was never reached.

Others would try to add a percentage for risk which depended on the nature of the compensation event. Here risk is at least identified. Agreement on the level of the appropriate percentage for the risks was not always possible and, more often than not, the work had been done before agreement had been reached.

On a number of sites, the *Project Manager* would identify risk by stating it as an assumption. The *Contractor*, while developing the quotation, would often identify others and seek clarification from the *Project Manager*. By identifying, analysing and developing management strategies for risks an approximate figure could be agreed for the cost of the risk should they occur. This was then divided by the likelihood of it occurring. The *Project Manager* would then relate this figure to the *Employer's* desire for certainty versus potential for least cost and take a view on whether the *Employer* wished to take the risk or allocate it to the *Contractor*.

A word of warning: risk assessment is an imprecise science. On one site the quantity surveyors representing the *Employer* would want the management strategy for mitigating the effect of a risk, should it occur, to be priced with the same rigour as the main body of the compensation event (and they would discuss it in detail), only for it to be divided by an arbitrary figure for the likelihood of it occurring. This caused considerable frustration to the *Contractor*, who was not being reimbursed for the cost of preparing quotations (see comments in the next section and in Appendix 2 on clause 11.2 (28)). For the above system to work with agreement to be reached prior to the work proceeding, it does depend on the *Contractor* being realistic in his risk allowances and for the those representing the *Employer* to see risk from the *Contractor's* viewpoint. If this is the case, all can benefit.

On one contract, a compensation event occurred which was likely to cause disruption to work specified in the original

Works Information. The *Contractor* could have included this disruption as a time risk allowance (with the resulting costs) in his quotation. Instead, he offered to take this risk for a premium, which was discussed and agreed. If the disruption occurred, the *Contractor* undertook to bear the cost of keeping the progress of the works on programme. The *Project Manager* compared this premium with the *Employer's* objectives and included this figure in the quotation. The *Contractor* was then motivated to manage the disruption which he did, rather than take advantage of the *Employer's* misfortune which would be the classical situation for claims management on conventional construction contracts.

The change in the Contractor's *method of working and resources*
Having gone through the previous stages, the most efficient and effective way of implementing the compensation event can be formulated. As the *Employer* is paying for the compensation event and there is a lack of competition, he is entitled to have a say, usually via the *Project Manager*, in how the work will be done. However, it should be remembered that the *Contractor* has been employed because of his expertise in construction and this can and should be used to develop a more economic and timely solution. A number of *Contractors* commented that their expertise is traditionally under utilised in the management of variations and that they liked being able to contribute to solving problems. An ideal way of encouraging this is to pay for time spent preparing and considering quotations. This goes against clause 11.2 (28) of Options A and B of the ECC which excludes the cost of preparing quotations from Actual Cost. Under the first edition of the NEC, the situation was unclear, but those who did reimburse the *Contractor's* cost of preparing quotations considered it money well spent (see Appendix 2).

Before proceeding with the detailed pricing of different methods for dealing with the compensation events, it may be beneficial for the *Contractor* to give ball park estimates, so that the *Project Manager* requests quotations for economic solutions. A problem with this is that once a price is mentioned, people have a tendency to become emotional if the detailed quotation then exceeds this amount. This occurred on a couple of projects within the research sample.

Once the most economic, timely or risk free method of working has been agreed, then the changes from the original method of working can be compared with those in the Accepted Programme. From this, the change in the total quantity (amount multiplied by duration) of labour and Equipment, and of Plant and Materials that are directly involved in the activity can be calculated. This emphasises the need for the *Project Manager* to study the method statements and resources for each operation which the *Contractor* is required to supply in a submitted programme. Any disruption and consequent loss of productivity arising from the compensation event which indirectly affect other activities should also be taken into account.

The change to the overall duration of the contract

If it is a significant compensation event then Completion of the contract may be delayed, and hence the Completion Date will be put back by the same time. The indirect resources which are to be kept on site longer (traditionally referred to as preliminaries) need to be identified. It is worthwhile noting again that, under the current Shorter Schedule of Cost Components, the *Contractor* will only be paid for a percentage applied to his people costs for the items in all of **Charges** 4. Under the normal Schedule of Cost Components, he will only be paid for the percentage applied to his people costs for the items in **Charges** 44. If the *Contractor* has only allowed for additional use of these items (i.e. quantity related costs) and not additional hire costs (i.e. time related costs), then it is questionable if he will fully recover his costs (see section 3.2.3 for a fuller explanation).

The change in Actual Costs related to each of the last three headings
With the exception of risk, where the figure will be less clear cut, if the previous stages have been followed, then it is should merely be a question of putting costs to the changed resources and adding them up to gain the total change in Actual Costs to which the *fee percentage* is applied. If the users have a Contract Cost Manual or, on smaller sites, have pre-agreed the cost of individual resources then it is a simple and quick matter of arithmetic (see 'Other tips' at the end of this section).

Communication and iteration
A feature in the majority of projects in the research sample was that the *Contractor* was given initial parameters and assumptions to prepare the compensation event quotation and there would then be little or no consultation with the *Project Manager* or the quantity surveyors representing him until the quotation was submitted. At this point, the *Project Manager* would see the final figure for the first time, think it was high (and bear in mind that most people are only used to seeing direct costs during the construction phase, with delay and disruption costs being covered in the claim which is determined after construction) and ask the *Contractor* to resubmit the quotation. Consequently, much of the detailed work was abortive because, for instance, productivity and risks had not been agreed. Having been asked to resubmit the quotation, it was only then that the two parties would discuss and agree these principles, and, having done so, the next formal quotation submission by the *Contractor* was agreed informally. It is clear to the author that interim discussions before the first formal submission of the quotation would have been beneficial in almost all circumstances. This is really an extension of the collaborative working principle that runs through the ECC.

This did happen on some contracts, with the *Employer's* and *Contractor's* quantity surveyors sitting in the same office and working out quotations together. They would reach agreement on each of the previously mentioned headings before considering the next. That is not to say there was no iteration — for instance, a risk may emerge when considering the method of doing the work. On a tunnelling project, the two planners representing the *Employer* and *Contractor* would agree the programme effects, from which changes in costs flow, before passing the financial assessment and detail onto their quantity surveyors to agree. When this was done, it meant that the acceptance of the final quotation was almost a formality by the time it was submitted, resulting in less time, effort and acrimony in agreeing the quotation and a greater likelihood that both parties can achieve the benefits outlined at the start of this section.

Other tips

- On smaller sites with fewer workmen, it is suggested that the Actual Costs of the individual workmen are agreed in the post award phase. On larger sites, a quotation manual can be agreed which subsumes the Schedule of Cost Components. This details the standard costs for different types of Equipment and categories of workman. It should also be agreed which workmen fit into which category. When a compensation event occurs, having agreed the units of time worked of Equipment and People, it is then simply a matter of multiplying time by cost per unit time.
- Where the compensation event involves additional design by the *Contractor*, it may be helpful to split the compensation event into two parts to conform to the time scales for submission of quotations of the ECC. The first is for the additional design and the second for the additional physical work. Problems will still be encountered with the second part, when there is no original drawing with which to compare the revised design. This, however, is one of the problems with design and build under any form of contract.
- In some circumstances, the effects of a compensation event may be too uncertain even for assumptions to be stated. Two strategies are suggested, either
    - the work proceeds with records being taken until the uncertainty is reduced to a level where assumptions can be stated with reasonable accuracy, or

- o   the compensation event is broken down into chunks, e.g. in a tunnel, unexpected physical conditions are encountered, so the *Contractor* is asked for a quotation for the next 100 metres of boring as opposed to the whole of the remaining tunnel.
- The general pattern encountered in the research was the more realistic the initial quotation, the more likely it was to be accepted first time. This gives the *Contractor* a cash flow advantage — as the sooner the quotation is accepted (and the work done), the sooner the *Contractor* is paid. Where the initial quotations were 20–30% over that expected by the *Project Manager*, he would generally evaluate the quotation in detail and in the process of negotiation and clarification, any profit outside the *fee percentage* would be taken out. The *Contractor* would then be instructed to submit the revised quotation which had in effect already been agreed. On the few sites where the *Contractor* consistently submitted unjustifiably high quotations, the *Project Manager* would eventually lose patience and start to impose his own assessments on the *Contractor* to the overall detriment of the *Contractor*. The recommendation is that it is not in any party's interests for the *Contractor* to consistently submit quotations for compensation events which are known by him to be excessive.

The author is aware of three large compensation events, where there was a significant difference between the change in Actual Costs worked out using the Schedule of Cost Components and the real change in the *Contractor's* cost.[*] This was to the *Contractor's* advantage in one of the cases and to the *Employer's* on the other two and was predominantly due to the deficiencies in the Schedule of Cost Components highlighted in section 3.2.3. In these cases, the injured party protested sufficiently strongly and the other party listened. Having satisfied themselves of the authenticity of the

---

[*] There were other cases, but these were either due to the *Contractor* being unable to justify the change in his resources due to a poor Accepted Programme or a lack of realism in the various percentages tendered.

Contractor's case and that the internal hire rates were competitive, an agreement was reached which satisfied both parties.

On one large site, the cost of *Contractor*-owned tracked cranes was worked out to be a few pounds per hour using the normal Schedule of Cost Components which was much less than the site was paying their own plant hire company. The *Contractor* threatened to off-hire the existing cranes and bring in different ones from an external company because they would be losing so much money. Once the quantity surveyors representing the *Employer* had satisfied themselves that the *Contractor's* internal hire rate was competitive, this was the rate that was paid.

3.5.5 *Use of the* Adjudicator

The procedures of the ECC should decrease the likelihood of conflict developing and the need to refer individual disputes to the *Adjudicator* when compared to other conditions of contract. Within the research sample, only two matters were referred to adjudication. Certainly, in the early use of the ECC, adjudication was a rare occurrence. However, disputes will inevitably occur on some contracts.

The procedure in the second edition does not comply with the Housing Grants, Construction and Regeneration Act 1996 (Part II), but would apply anywhere outside England and Wales. An addendum, Secondary Option Y(UK)2, was issued by the Institution of Civil Engineers in April 1998 so that the payment and adjudication provisions of the ECC comply with the Act.

Under clause 90.1 of the unamended contract, the *Contractor* has to notify a dispute over any action or inaction of the *Project Manager* or *Supervisor* to the *Project Manager* within four weeks of that action or inaction. Between two and four weeks after this notification, the dispute may be submitted to the *Adjudicator*. For any other matter, either party may submit a dispute to the *Adjudicator* between two and four weeks after the notification to the other Party and the *Project Manager*. If a party is dissatisfied with the *Adjudicator's* decision, they have four weeks to notify the other of their intention to refer the matter to the *tribunal* (arbitration, litigation, executive tribunal etc. as specified in the Contract Data) (clause 93.1). Failure to observe these time scales effectively means that the party is time barred from taking the dispute on to the *tribunal*. The *tribunal* proceedings cannot start until after Completion.

The Housing Grants, Construction and Regeneration Act (1996) effectively outlawed the ECC's procedures in England and Wales by saying that a dispute has to be referable to the *Adjudicator* 'at any time'. This could allow a *Contractor* to do a cost reconciliation at the end of a contract and go to Adjudication to try and recover some of the difference between income and expenditure. The authors of the ECC have attempted to partly circumvent this provision by saying that before any matter becomes a dispute, the dissatisfied Party has to notify the *Project Manager* of his dissatisfaction within four weeks of the action, inaction or when they became aware of the matter (amended clauses 90.2 and 90.3). Within two weeks of the notification, the Parties and the *Project Manager* have a meeting to discuss and resolve the matter (amended clause 90.3) and that 'no matter shall become a dispute unless a notice of dissatisfaction has been given and the matter has not been resolved within four weeks' (amended clause 90.4). Like the unamended clauses, if a party is dissatisfied with the decision, they have four weeks to notify the other of their intention to refer the matter to the *tribunal* and the *tribunal* proceedings cannot start until after Completion.

The research corroborated findings from America:[*]

---

[*] Rowley F. (1996). Engineer demise, adjudicator rise. *New Civil Engineer*, 14th Nov.

- Adjudication is rarely used as the parties perceive that they have failed if they have to use it.
- If a dispute is referred to the *Adjudicator*, it is rare for it to proceed beyond this stage.

Other observations which give a greater incentive for the parties to resolve the matter themselves within the time scales are that

- once a dispute is referred to the *Adjudicator*, the parties have lost the ability to manage and influence the outcome
- under the ECC, the *Adjudicator's* decision has to be fairly cut and dried. In practice, disputes are often more complicated. Both those who 'won' the decision and those who conducted the Adjudication noted this.
- the referred matter was the tip of the iceberg. In the two disputes in the research sample, the *Contractor* was not happy generally with the *Project Manager's* decisions and was almost looking for an excuse to make a point. The decision therefore only addressed the symptoms of the dispute and not the underlying cause.

For these reasons, some participants suggested that the *Adjudicator* should be encouraged to act in a more conciliatory role, trying to make the Parties accommodate and understand each other's views, and only give a decision when all else has failed. This role is not facilitated by the words in the main contract or by the NEC Adjudicator's contract.

3.6 CONCLUSIONS TO PART III

The ECC is as much a tool for project managing a contract as a condition of contract. Like most tools, its effectiveness depends on how it is used by people. People therefore need the skills and attitude to use it as intended by its authors. In terms of skills, as one *Employer's* contracts manager stated, what is needed from all parties are 'estimators not quantity surveyors, planners or claims consultants' i.e. the ability to use skills pro-actively, rather than with the benefit of hindsight. The cultural aspect also reflects this, but on the *Employer's* side, an acceptance is needed that the *Contractor* is entitled to a fair profit if he plays a constructive part in the construction process. If the *Employer* sets the scene and then confirms this attitude with his actions, more often than not it will be returned by the *Contractor*. As one *Contractor's* agent stated: 'if your profit margin is largely secure, why play the games? It simply undermines the ethos of the contract'.

To summarise, to secure his profit, the *Contractor* needs to ensure that

- the Prices submitted for the work detailed in the Works Information are accurate (section 3.2.1)
- the various percentages tendered in the Contract Data Part II are correct (section 3.2.4) — which, the author admits, the current structure of the Schedule of Cost Components does not always facilitate (section 3.2.3)
- the right quantity and quality of personnel involved in the contract, who have the appropriate skills and attitude are selected (section 3.1.3)
- training appropriate to the personnel involved on the 'why' and 'how' the contract is conducted (section 3.4.1)
- a good programme is submitted and maintained throughout the contract from which the *Project Manager* can clearly see where the *Contractor's* costs come, so that the cost and time effects of compensation events can easily be determined (sections 3.2.2 and 3.4.2) and the *Contractor* works that programme throughout the contract
- a system of pro-formas is in place at the start of the contract to minimise administration (section 3.4.3)
- early warnings are given as a matter of policy (section 3.5.2)
- procedures are in place and staffing levels are adequate to respond within the time scales of the ECC, especially in the submission of quotations for compensation events (sections 3.5.3 and 3.5.4).

The benefits of the above, according to interviewees in the research sample, are improved cash flow, faster settlement of the final account and a more assured profit margin. On five contracts within the research sample, *Contractors* managed to increase their expected profit margin by between 3 and 4% on turnover. This was done by

- placing greater emphasis on pro-active programming, which the ECC encourages
- having supplied a good Accepted Programme, working with the *Project Manager* to reduce time and costs and being allowed to retain some of the benefits if this is not predetermined by the payment option
- preparing quotations alongside the *Project Manager* or his representative, so that the *Project Manager* is effectively rubber stamping them when they are formally submitted
- prioritising the assessment and agreement of compensation events where the physical work had not yet been done, including taking some of the risk, so that they could reap the financial rewards if they managed it well, rather than assessing compensation events from records.

The last two points give improved cash flow which in turn increases profit. On these contracts, people representing the *Employer* did not begrudge the *Contractor* their additional profit, but more felt it was a just reward for their positive contribution i.e. it was not made at the expense of the *Employer*.

What does the *Employer* and his team need to do to gain the most from using the ECC? Clearly defined objectives and an appropriate level of risk management, both of which are reflected in an appropriate contract strategy (section 1.3) and good quality documentation (section 3.1.1), all increase the likelihood of a project meeting its objectives. However, this is true of any project, it is just that the ECC has greater flexibility compared to traditional conditions of contract. In most ways, it is matching the *Contractor's* inputs. For instance

- ensuring that the Prices and various percentages accepted at tender are realistic (section 3.3)
- training appropriate to the personnel involved (section 3.4.1)

- having the right quantity and quality of personnel involved in the contract, who have the appropriate skills and attitude (section 3.1.3)
- putting in place a system of pro-formas and procedures to ensure time scales are adhered to (section 3.4.3)
- being willing to use the ECC's system of sanctions if necessary to encourage best practice, but if using them, doing so in a constructive manner e.g. if the programme sanctions are used, then critique the programme so that the *Contractor* knows what has to be done for it to be accepted
- working with the *Contractor*, so he can fulfil his objectives, because that, in turn, helps the *Employer* achieve his objectives. This can include analysing the *Contractor's* programme to see what the *Employer* can do to save time and cost, working along side the *Contractor* when he is preparing quotations, seeing risk from a *Contractor's* point of view, prioritising the assessment of compensation events where the physical work has not yet been done and being prepared to share with the *Contractor* some of the benefits arising from efficient work (although this is not as easily done under the price-based Options A and B).

The main advantages of using the NEC/ECC to *Employers*, according to interviewees in the research sample, were a greater knowledge of where the contract is heading in terms of time and cost and, armed with this knowledge, a greater ability to influence the outcome. On contracts subject to a large degree of change in scope or method of working during the contract, both those representing the *Employer* and *Contractor* thought that the use of the NEC/ECC saved the *Employer* money because of the increased communication and planning that occurred prior to the physical work proceeding. On three contracts, participants thought that the use of the NEC/ECC brought forward the achievement of the time deadline — indeed on one, an interviewee said that he could not have foreseen the contract being completed to the time deadline under any other conditions of contract. Faster settlement of final account was also consistently mentioned as an advantage.

The contracts thought to be most successful by participants were the ones where the procedures, clauses and time scales of the contract were adhered to, albeit not slavishly. On these contracts, to comply with the ECC and its spirit and intent, the procedures and processes outlined in this book were all evident to varying degrees.

Author's Note
Research into various aspects of the ECC continues at the University of Birmingham, with the object of both improving the contract and insights into how to use it most effectively. Should users wish to comment or discuss the contents of this book or contribute their experiences for further research, please feel free to contact me at the School of Civil Engineering, The University of Birmingham, Birmingham, B15 2TT, United Kingdom. At the time of going to press my contact details are as follows. Tel: 07970 428929; E-mail: jonybroome@aol.com.

Appendix 1

Model pro-forma sheets

As suggested in section 3.4.3, these pro-formas should be used as the base for individuals to tailor pro-formas for their individual contract.

TECHNICAL ENQUIRY (TQ)

Contract:	Contract No.:

Date:	TQ No:
	Previous relevant communications:

Section A
To: the Project Manager

Additional information and/or
clarification is needed regarding:
(a) drawing no.: ....
(b) specification section: ....

Category:
    Technical Query/Resolution

    Alternative Proposal

    Notification of Possible CE

    Early Warning

Copy To:

PROPOSAL OR RESOLUTION IF APPROPRIATE

Signed for Contractor:	Title: ....

Distribute to (For comments prior to response):	Responses needed by: ....

Section B: Response. To: the Contractor	Copy To:
	Title: ....
Signed for Employer:	Date: ....

CONTRACTOR'S SUBMISSION (CS)

Contract:	Contract No.:

Date:	Submission No.: CS
Discipline:	Revision No.:
Specification Section:	Previous relevant communications:

To: the Project Manager/Supervisor
Copies To:

Submission for Acceptance of:

Drawing
Programme
Test Results

The following is transmitted for your review and acceptance:

COPIES	DATE	No.	DESCRIPTION

Distribute to
(For comments prior to response):

Responses needed by: ....

To: The Contractor's Agent:
The Submission is returned as indicated:

Accepted	Accepted as Noted
Revise and Re-submit as Noted	Rejected as Noted

Notes:

Reviewed by:	Signed by: ....
Title: .... Date:	Title: .... Date: ....

PROJECT MANAGER'S INSTRUCTION (PMI)

Contract:	Contract No.:

Category:
  General Instruction
  Instruction changing Works
    Information
  Proposal to change Works
    Information
	Instruction No.: PMI
	Revision No.:
	Date:
	Previous relevant communications:

ITEM   DESCRIPTION

Commence work immediately Advise within ...... days of any time/ cost impact Keep records	Instruction issued as a change proposal for your return within .... days Do not start work No cost instruction

Signed by: ....
Title: .... Date: ....
	Copies To: Civils
	  Employer M&E
	  Architect Landscape
	  Structural Other:

Note: This is a summary sheet. The impact of each individual item should be identified on supporting documentation	Contractor's Summary 1. Impact on Programme is plus .... days/weeks or none
Signed for the Contractor: .... Title: .... Date:	2. Impact on Actual Cost plus Fee is: plus £ .... minus £ .... none ....

Copies to (Contractor's Employees/Subcontractors):

COMPENSATION EVENT (CE)

Contract	Contract No.:

To:	Notification	CE No.:
Previous relevant communications:	Implementation	Date:

In accordance with the Conditions of Contract you are notified of the compensation event described below.

The work described below has been assessed as a compensation event. The nett changes to the cost and programme together with the new Contract Price and Completion Date are indicated below. The compensation event is now implemented.

Description of Work

Is this a Project Manager's assessment imposed on the Contractor: Yes/No

Cost Summary:	Programme Summary:
Contract Sum prior to CE: £	Original Completion Date: ....
Add/Deduct: £	Add/Deduct: .... Mnths ....Wks .... Days
New Contract Prices: £	**New Completion Date:** ....

Signed by:	Copies To:	Civils
	Employer	M&E
Title: .... Date:	Architect	Landscape
	Structural	Other:

Copies to (Contractor's Employees/Subcontractors):

SUPERVISOR'S NOTIFICATION (SN)

Contract:		Contract No.:
Sheet No.: SN	Previous Relevant Sheets:	Date:

To: the *Contractor* with copies to   the Project Manager
Others:

Type of Notification/Instruction: Date   Time
  Notification of test or inspection to be done on   .... at ....
  Notification of result of test or inspection done on .... at ....
      Was the test or inspection passed: YES/NO
  Notification of a Defect discovered on   .... at ....
  Instruction to Search:
      Is this a Result of Lack of Sufficient Notice by *Contractor*: Yes/No

Location and Details:

Signed by: .... Print Name: ....

Test/Inspection Done On: _ _ / _ _ / _ _ at _ _ . _ _ . Test: PASSED/FAILED
If failed, reason for failure:

Other Comments:

Signed by: .... Print Name: ....

Defect corrected on:
Next relevant sheet No.:

CONTRACTOR'S NOTIFICATION TO SUPERVISOR (CN)

Contract: Contract No.:

Sheet No.: CN	Previous Relevant Sheets:	Date:

To: the *Supervisor* with copies to:
  the *Project Manager*
  Subcontractors:
  Others:

Type of Notification: Date   Time
  Notification of test or inspection to be done on   .... at ....
  Notification of result of test or inspection done on .... at ....
  Notification of a Defect discovered on   .... at ....

Details:

Signed by: .... Print Name: ....

Other Comments (tick as appropriate):
  It is planned to correct the Defect and re-test/inspect on (date) ....
  The *Contractor* will propose to the *Project Manager* that the Works
Information will be changed in return for a reduction in the Prices and/or
Completion Date.

Next relevant sheet No.:

Appendix 2

Suggestions for modifications to the second edition of the NEC Engineering and Construction Contract

These are the author's personal suggestions for the main areas of the ECC that users may wish to alter depending on the project circumstances. It uses two sources: feedback from users both within the research sample and since its conclusion, and comments of lawyers. Its objectives are threefold, namely

- to close any more obvious legal loopholes
- to further stimulate good management
- to make the contract more workable without users being in danger of breach of contract. In this sense it makes legitimate what people have been doing in practice.

Clause	Comment/Alteration
11.2 (2)	Insert ', notified or accepted by the *Project Manager*,' after organisations. This prevents the *Contractor* having to co-operate with, for example environmental protesters under clause 25.1.
11.2 (28) in Options A & B	In the first edition, it was unclear who paid for the cost of assessing the compensation events. This was clarified in the second edition: it is the *Contractor*. Under the first edition, on those sites where the *Contractor* was reimbursed for his time, the *Project Manager* thought he gained value as the *Contractor* was willingly using his management expertise to decrease the direct costs of the compensation event. Other reasons for allocating the cost to the *Employer* are:

- a compensation event is an *Employer's* risk. It is inconsistent to allocate only this aspect of that risk to the *Contractor*.
- the *Employer* ultimately pays for the cost of assessing compensation events, but it is currently hidden elsewhere in the *Contractor's* Prices or *fee percentage*. Lack of transparency does not aid co-operation.
- if the cost of assessing compensation events is in the Prices, then the *Contractor* is guessing at this cost as he does not know and cannot control the extent of compensation events
- the cost of assessing compensation events is not directly proportional to the cost of the compensation event. Therefore, the size of the *fee percentage* may not reflect the *Contractor's* costs in assessing that particular compensation event.
- if the cost of assessing compensation events is allocated to the *Contractor*, then it encourages

Clause	Comment/Alteration

abuse by the *Project Manager*. For instance, asking for numerous quotations or excessive detail.

If the *Contractor* is not being reimbursed his true costs for events which are beyond his control, this does not aid team spirit. For all of these reasons, allocating this cost to the *Contractor* can, and has in certain cases, resulted in some ill-feeling at site level.

16.5   Users may wish to insert a new clause which requires those on site to have periodic early warning meetings to ensure minor matters are resolved as the project progresses.

3   The NEC and ECC is a major advance over other contracts in its programming provisions and how they are incorporated into the working of the contract. However, depending on the project circumstances, changes may be desirable

- in order to accommodate the concepts of multi-level planning (section 3.1.2). For instance, it is not necessary for a short term programme to show all the information detailed in clause 31.2.
- as the ECC is weak for management-based contracts as it does not allow late alterations to the times in which works contractors can work without it being a compensation event. So, if one works contractor delays the work of another, the second can justifiably notify a compensation event, but the *Employer* (under the construction management approach) or *Contractor* (under the management contracting approach) cannot set off the costs of the compensation event against the works contractor. *Contractors* may wish to alter the subcontract for similar reasons.

Clause	Comment/Alteration

45.1 Replace 'assesses' with 'may assess'

54.3 If the *Employer* wishes to affect the *Contractor's activity schedule*, then this is the clause to ensure, that having won the contract, the *Contractor* does not alter the *activity schedule* satisfying only the first three bullet points of this clause. An additional bullet point stating that 'it does not comply with the requirements of the Works Information' can be added. The requirements could be to reflect cash flow constraints acting on the project, payments for achieving performance e.g. in projects involving software, or to limit the number of activities in the *activity schedule* (section 3.2.2). However, there are dangers in the *Employer* over-specifying how the *Contractor* puts together his *activity schedule* and this suggestion needs to be used wisely.

60.1 (4) This clauses makes it a compensation event if the *Project Manager* stops the work for any reason. The author would suggest that he should be allowed to stop a part of the *works*, without it being a compensation event, if the reason is because the *Contractor* is not complying with the contract or the applicable law. However, clause 61.4 does state that the Prices and Completion Date are not changed if a compensation event, notified by the *Contractor*, arises from a fault of the *Contractor*.

61.3 The implication of the second bullet point of clause 61.3 is that a compensation event is deemed not to exist if the *Contractor* has not notified it within two weeks of becoming aware of it (although the *Project Manager* can notify a compensation event at any time). The intention is to prevent *Contractors* coming to the end of the contract, doing a cost/

Clause	Comment/Alteration

income reconciliation and putting forward lots of compensation events to make up the difference. Potential users may wish to make this an explicit statement, by adding an additional bullet point to the first set of bullet points in clause 61.4.

62.2   The last sentence of this clause may be inoperable where the frequency of compensation events is high as it would mean a new programme is submitted every time there is a minor compensation event. There are two ways around this, namely

(a) 'the programme for remaining work is affected' could be replaced by 'Completion is changed' or 'the Completion Date is changed', or

(b) a statement could be added to the effect that if the *Project Manager* and *Contractor* agree, the effect of a single or group of minor compensation events can be evaluated in the next revision of the programme.

64.1   Replace 'assesses' with 'may assess' in the first line of this clause. This gives the *Project Manager* some leeway to exercise common sense if the *Contractor* is slightly late for a good reason. For instance, a large number of compensation events occur in a short period.

90.1   In both the standard conditions and the Y2.5 (the amendments to comply with the Housing Grants, Construction and Regeneration Act (1996) in the UK), it may be worthwhile, adding that for the purposes of the Adjudication clauses, a communication of the *Project Manager* is deemed to be an action.

Clause	Comment/Alteration
Option L and Option R	Valentine (see Appendix 3) notes that the application of delay damages for the whole of the *works* becomes unclear when damages are also levied on sections of the *works*. This concerns the wording used in the Contract Data Part I. Care needs to be taken that damages do not become punitive.
SCC	Both Schedules of Cost Components are structured so that, in certain circumstances, the way in which costs are built up do not match how the *Contractor* incurs costs on site (section 3.2.3). There are some other anomalies: for instance, why is it only Equipment where the *Contractor* is not reimbursed for up to a half-day (under the normal method) of idle or standby time and not People? Additionally, as a number of interviewees within the research sample commented, the standards of clarity do not match those set in the main contract conditions.

Appendix 3

Bibliography

Legal commentaries include:

Cornes D. L. (1996). The second edition of the New Engineering Contract. *The Int. Construction Law Review*, **13**, Part 1, 97–119.

Egglestone B. (1996). *The New Engineering Contract: a Commentary*, Blackwell Science Ltd, Oxford.

Valentine D. G. (1996). The New Engineering Contract
- Part 1: a new language
- Part 2: claims for extensions of time
- Part 3: late completion and liquidated damages.

Construction Law J., **12**, 5, Sweet & Maxwell, London.

Two useful, but similar, commentaries on implementing the ECC across an organisation are:

Baird A. (1994). The New Engineering Contract — a management summary for plant industry users. *The Int. Construction Law Review*, **11**, Part 2, 114–127.

Baird A. (1995). Pioneering the NEC system of documents. *Engineering, Construction and Architectural Management*, **2**, Part 4, 249–269.

Any paper or article by Barnes M. or Perry J. G. on the subject of contracts will provide useful insight into the philosophy and thinking behind the ECC. For instance:

Barnes M. (1983). How to allocate risks in construction contracts. *The Int. J. of Project Management*, **1**, 1, 24–28.
Barnes M. (1987). Prevention is better than dispute. *The Int. Construction Law Review*, **4**, 3, 295–301.
Perry J. G. (1995). The New Engineering Contract: principles of design and risk allocation. *Engineering, Construction and Architectural Management*, **2**, 3, 197–208.

Published papers by this author include:

Broome J. C. and Perry J. G. (1995). Experiences of the use of the New Engineering Contract. *Engineering, Construction and Architectural Management*, **2**, 4, 271–286.
Broome J. C. (1997). Best practice with the New Engineering Contract. *Proc. Civil Engineering*, Institution of Civil Engineers, May. Thomas Telford Ltd, London.
Broome J. C. and Hayes R. W. (1997). A comparison of the clarity of traditional construction contracts and of the New Engineering Contract. *Int. J. of Project Management*, **15**, 4, Aug.

The author has also written a series of articles which appear in the NEC Users Newsletter from Issue No. 7, Winter 1996/1997 onwards.

Appendix 4

Quick reference guide to terminology of the NEC Engineering and Construction Contract

This quick reference guide is to enable readers to assimilate the key terms used in the ECC. It is not intended as a legal interpretation of their meaning or consequences.

Contract Data: Contract specific data is referenced in the main contract by the use of italicised terms or by specific reference to the Contract Data. Part I is filled in by the *Employer* when issuing his enquiry and Part II by the *Contractor* when returning his tender.

The *Employer* and *Contractor*: the Parties to the contract.

The *Project Manager*: the person appointed to manage the contract on the *Employer's* behalf.

The *Supervisor*: the person appointed to check quality on the *Employer's* behalf.

The *Adjudicator*: an independent third party brought in to resolve disputes quickly which cannot be resolved by the parties and above characters.

Works Information: the part of the specification which

- specifies and describes the *works* i.e. what the *Contractor* has to do
- states any constraints on how the *Contractor* is to Provide the Works.

Site Information: the part of the documentation which describes the Site and its surroundings.

The Working Areas: the Site (described by the *Employer*) and any additional areas used by the *Contractor* to Provide the Works. These are either stated in the Contract Data Part I or proposed by the *Contractor* and accepted by the *Project Manager*.

Plant and Materials: items intended to be included in the *works*.

Equipment: construction plant and temporary works.

Completion: the date on which the *Contractor* actually completes the work which the contract states he has to do before the Completion Date.

Completion Date: the date on or before which the *Contractor* has to achieve Completion in order to avoid damages for delay.

The Accepted Programme: the latest programme which has been submitted to and accepted by the *Project Manager* as satisfying the criteria stated in the contract and Works Information.

Early warning: a contractual procedure for either the *Project Manager* or *Contractor* to notify the other of any matter which could increase the Prices, delay Completion or impair the performance of the *works* in use.

Early warning meeting: a meeting which may be held after an early warning notice to consider options and agree measures to minimise the effects of notified matter.

The *defects date* is a stated period after Completion in which Defects can be notified to the *Contractor*.

The *defects correction period*: the period, from Completion until the *defects date*, which the *Contractor* has to correct a Defect once it is notified.

The Prices: precise definition varies between the main options. Essentially, the total of the Prices is the most up-to-date estimate (of contractual standing) of what the *Employer* will eventually pay — plus or minus the *Employer's* share of cost over or under run ·on the target cost options.

The Price for Work Done To Date: precise definition varies between the main options. Essentially, it is the predominant component of the amount paid to the *Contractor* for work done up to a particular date.

Actual Cost: precise definition varies between the main options. Except for Option F, it references and incorporates the Schedule of Cost Components into the contract.

The Schedule of Cost Components (SCC): A list of items at the back of the contract for which the *Contractor* is reimbursed if there is a compensation event under the priced options (A and B) and for all costs, other than subcontracted work, under the cost-based options (C, D and E). There are two schedules, the normal SCC and the Shorter Schedule of Cost Components, with the latter being used for the assessment of simpler compensation events.

The *fee percentage*: the percentage tendered by the *Contractor* which is applied to Actual Costs. It is deemed to include whatever is not included in Actual Cost e.g. profit, off-site overheads and insurances.

Compensation events: a list of events for which the *Employer* is liable and which, if they occur, may entitle the *Contractor* to additional time and money.

Index

costs
    post-specification changes 53–54, 91
    quotation-preparation 80
cross referencing, lack in NEC/ECC
    10, 94

day-to-day management 35, 103
    see also Supervisor
daywork rates 131–132
defect correction period 39, 40, 55
    meaning of term 39, 185
Defect(s)
    accepting 55
    correcting 37, 39, 55
    meaning of term 39
    notifying 39
    and tests/inspections 55
    uncorrected 40
Defects Certificate 39–40
defects date 39, 109, 184
defined terms 34, 36–37
definitions, potential confusion 10–11
delay damages (Option R) 26, 37
    suggested modification to ECC
    180
Delay/delay, and compensation events
    24
delegation, by *Project Manager* 35,
    102
depreciation and maintenance rates
    (for Equipment in SCC) 123–124
design
    Contractor's 28–29
    Employer's 35, 75
design-and-build contract 28, 37
designers 35
Disallowed Cost 42
dispute ladder 112
disputes
    avoidance and resolution of 35,
    58–59, 112, 161
    cost to industry 57
    ECC designed to minimise 57–59,
    65, 160
dissatisfaction
    notification of 161

time allowed for resolution 161
documentation 53
    deficiencies made more apparent
    92
    preparation of 91–98
    see also Site Information; Works
    Information
drafting philosophy (for NEC) 12–13
Dwyer, Steve 85

early Completion bonus 26
early warning
    effects 45, 56, 69
    responsibility 44–45, 83, 163
early warning meeting 45, 73, 77, 144
    meaning of term 45, 184
    records 45, 77, 144
    suggested modification to ECC
    177
early warning procedure 44–45, 56,
    69, 77, 144
    example of use 144–145
    meaning of term 44–45, 184
ECC: *see* NEC Engineering and
    Construction Contract
ECS: *see* NEC Engineering and
    Construction Subcontract
Employer
    actions required 34
    advanced payment by 26
    advantages of NEC/ECC for
    164–166
    and compensation events 45, 176
    Contract Data 101–114
    and *Contractor's* design 28–29
    division of work into segments
    120
    experience of ECC 62–65
    facilities and services provided by
    93
    good-management stimulus 50–51
    information on Site conditions 45
    management of contract 34, 183
    meaning of term 34, 183
    as Party to contract 34, 183
    responsibilities 92, 164–165

limitations when used in
 construction management
 approach   68, 90
modifications suggested   175–180
overview   33–48
as stimulus to good management
 13, 48–59
NEC Engineering Construction Short
 Contract   6, 9, 69
NEC Engineering and Construction
 Subcontract (ECS)   9
NEC Professional Services Contract
 5, 6, 9, 24, 35
New Engineering Contract
 history of development   4–6
 see also NEC...
nominated Subcontractors   8
notification
 compensation events   46, 57, 139,
  171, 178–179
 Defects   39
 of dissatisfaction   161

objectives, clearly defined   53
off-site overheads   128–129
open book accounting   14, 22, 73
open door policy for communications
 138–139
operations (in programme)   120
option clauses   9
 main options   16–25
 secondary options   25–28, 31, 35,
  160
 stated in Contract Data   102
Others (other people)
 co-operation with (clause 25.1)
  176
 definition, suggested modification to
  ECC   176

parent company guarantee (Option H)
 25
Parties/Party to contract   34–36, 183
partnering   14, 22, 78
 selection of personnel   104, 133
payment clauses   40–44

payment mechanisms   142–144
payment(s)
 advanced   26
 late   143
 by percentage completion   119
 promptness   51, 69, 73, 84, 86, 165
 terminology   40–44
 when to be made   143
 withholding   143
people costs
 rates in SCC   122–123, 156
 rates in Shorter SCC   126, 156
performance based activities, for
 maintenance contract   74
performance bond (Option G)   25, 26
performance impairment, early warning
 of possibility   44
performance specification, Works
 Information as   36
period for reply   37, 109
permanent works *see works*
personnel
 attitudes   103–104, 163–165
 quality of   53, 106, 163–165
 selection of   104, 133
 skills required   34, 105–107,
  163–165
physical conditions of the Site,
 boundary limits   95
plain English   10, 11, 69
plant, meaning of term   36
Plant and Materials
 manufacture or fabrication costs in
  SCC   125–126
 meaning of term   36, 184
 rates in SCC   124
post-award steps   134–142
 communications system
  development   137–142
 programme preparation   135–136
 training   134–135
potential problems, early
 identification   44–45, 56
pre-tender actions   91–116
 bill of quantities for *activity schedule*
  options   114–116